Especially for

....

From

....

Date

....

200 Nighttime
Prayers
for Women

Words of Comfort for a
Sweet, Peaceful Sleep

Emily Biggers

BARBOUR BOOKS
An Imprint of Barbour Publishing, Inc.

Our mission is to inspire the world with the life-changing message of the Bible.

Member of the
Evangelical Christian
Publishers Association

When you lie down, you will
not be afraid; when you lie down,
your sleep will be sweet.

PROVERBS 3:24 NIV

Introduction

If you are like most women today, you lead a busy life! You wear many hats from the time you wake up until the day ends. Starting your day in quiet time with God is always best. It sets the tone for your day, doesn't it? Just as important as getting off to a great start is finishing your day with your Creator and Lord. He created your body to require sleep. He values rest just as highly as work. Your heavenly Father longs to help you close your days wrapped in His arms of peace and comfort.

In this book you will find a short passage of scripture and a prayer starter to help you do just that each evening. Whether it is a reminder to leave your worries at the foot of His throne or encouragement to face your trials in His strength, you will find these entries helpful in your journey. So, get comfy and meet with the Lord as you meditate on His Word and bow before Him in prayer. Then drift off to peaceful sleep knowing that He sings over you (Zephaniah 3:17) and protects you (Psalm 4:8) through the night.

Songs in the Night

*But each day the Lord pours his
unfailing love upon me, and through
each night I sing his songs, praying
to God who gives me life.*

PSALM 42:8 NLT

Lord, You pour Your love upon me. I sense it
throughout each day. When I am up against
a trial, You are there—loving me. You give me
strength and wisdom. When I feel discouraged,
You lift me up. When I feel alone, You remind
me that You are always with me. I pause now
before I close this day, and I come before You
praising Your name. I praise You for who You
are. I give You all the glory. Father, I thank
You for Your goodness. You are the giver of all
good gifts. I thank You for all that You have done
and are doing in my life. I ask You to bless and
keep me through the night. I know that Your
mighty hand sustains my life. Thank You, Father.
In Jesus' name I pray, amen.

No Fear of the Night

Do not be afraid of the terrors of the night,
nor the arrow that flies in the day. Do not
dread the disease that stalks in darkness,
nor the disaster that strikes at midday.

PSALM 91:5–6 NLT

———◆———

God, You assure me that I need not fear the night. What comfort I find in this! As children we fear shadows and monsters. But when we grow into adults, our fears change. No longer do we shudder at every sound we hear, although I admit sometimes an unusual creak or clatter does still cause me fright at times! My anxieties and worries are different now, but every bit as strong. My giants come in the form of overdue bills. I worry about my family and my job. Teach me, Lord, to release these anxieties to You. I choose to rest in Your goodness and to allow You to protect me. You tell me in Your Word that You will fight for me. You tell me to have courage. In this world there is trouble, but You have overcome the world. Thank You for watching over me day and night. In Jesus' name I pray, amen.

Fire by Night

*He guided them with the cloud by day
and with light from the fire all night.*

PSALM 78:14 NIV

Lord, just as You guided the Israelites with fire all night long, I know that as I close this day, You are not going to sleep. You are well aware of my every need both day and night. You carry me through the day. I sense You not only in nature but in all of my interactions and dealings. Your Holy Spirit counsels me as I go about my work. When I encounter trouble, You never leave my side. You give me wisdom in handling it. And then, when the busyness of the day comes to an end, I meet with You here and You comfort me. You remind me that my identity is found in Christ alone and that I live and work and have my being for an audience of One. May I always look up, Father. May I find You in the cloud and in the fire. In Jesus' name, amen.

Security in God

In peace I will lie down and sleep,
for you alone, O LORD, will keep me safe.
PSALM 4:8 NLT

Lord, when I read this verse I envision a toddler playing all day long until she is worn out. Then, after a warm bath, she snuggles into warm pajamas and is rocked by her mother or father. They brush teeth and read stories. She says her prayers and drifts off to sleep in her bed, clutching a favorite stuffed bunny. It is the picture of security. It is the picture of peace. The child trusts completely in her parents to protect her. She feels safe in their arms. She is warm and comfortable. She is at rest. Father, this is how You want me to feel each night when I go to bed. You promise me that You will keep me safe through the night. You offer me peace that is found only in You. All I need to do is receive it. And so, I, like the toddler, lean into the strong chest of my Father tonight. I rest in You. In Jesus' name, amen.

God Sustains Me

*I lay down and slept, yet I woke up in safety,
for the LORD was watching over me.*

PSALM 3:5 NLT

Lord, You are the sustainer of life. You cause
the sun to rise again each new day. You provide
food for the animals and for Your children. You
created us, and You know our needs. You meet
them through the world You have given us to live
in. You have done so from the very beginning.
As I end this day, I am reminded of all the times
You came through for me today. Without You,
I would not have put my feet on the floor and
risen from my bed. I would not have drawn one
breath. You blessed me all day long, and You are
not going to stop even now. Through the night,
You will hold on to me. You will watch over me
and protect me. Lord, if it is Your will, I will
wake up again tomorrow morning. Go with me
through this night, I ask, and show Your favor
to me tomorrow that I might glorify You in all
that I do. Amen.

Jesus Is in Control

*The men were amazed, and said,
"What kind of a man is this, that even
the winds and the sea obey Him?"*

MATTHEW 8:27 NASB

Jesus, You were sleeping! The disciples were so frightened that night on the boat when the storm was raging. You called them men of little faith. I would have been one of them had I been there. I too find myself afraid during the storms of life. And yet, I take comfort in what You did next. You proved to them that You were fully in control the whole time. Certainly one who could calm the winds and the sea with just a word from His mouth would never have let His disciples perish in a storm! You may have had Your eyes closed, but You were never unaware. You were not about to let them drown at sea. Sometimes You choose to calm the storms that rage around me. Other times You carry me through them and protect me from the winds and rain. Either way, Savior, may I always trust in You. Give me peace as I go to sleep. Remind me that You are always in control. Amen.

Right on Time

So Jesus then said to them plainly,
"Lazarus is dead, and I am glad for your
sakes that I was not there, so that you
may believe; but let us go to him."

JOHN 11:14–15 NASB

———————

Lord, You are always right on time. Just as You showed up and raised Lazarus from the dead, You will show up and meet the needs in my life. Mary and Martha were worried and upset. They thought you had missed the chance to help their beloved brother. The disciples did not understand either. But You seized the opportunity to show them all that You were not late. You were just in time. Jesus, as I lay my head on my pillow tonight there are worries within me. I feel like I have been praying the same prayers for years. I keep bringing these requests before You, and it is easy to feel that You do not hear or You are not going to answer me. Help me to trust in You, Savior, and to realize that while Your timing may be different from my own, it is always best. Give me peace in the waiting, I ask. Amen.

Strength and Peace

The LORD will give strength to His people;
The LORD will bless His people with peace.

PSALM 29:11 NASB

Lord, You strengthen Your children. You gave David strength to fight the giant. You gave Noah strength to fight the laughter of the crowd as he built a giant ark upon dry land many miles from the sea. And You give me strength today to fight my own giants and my own naysayers. You bless Your people with peace. You gave Abraham peace as he climbed the mountain, believing he was called to sacrifice his son. You brought the raging storm to an instant halt and filled the disciples, weak in faith, with great peace that You were still in control. You give me peace in the midst of my storms and uncertainties today. Fill me with Your peace now as I go to sleep. Cause me to rest assured that You will never leave or forsake me. In Jesus' name, amen.

Set Free

"I am the LORD your God, who rescued you from the land of Egypt, the place of your slavery."

EXODUS 20:2 NLT

———◆———

Lord, just as You rescued the Israelites from Egypt, You have saved me from my place of slavery as well. No longer do I look to the world as my master. It does not rule over me in darkness any longer. I know a new master now. I live a new life filled with freedom the lost can only dream of experiencing. Keep me safe through this night, I pray, and cause me to rise up tomorrow ready to live out this freedom in a way that honors You. I want all of my days and all of my ways to serve as an altar constructed in Your honor. I will gaze upon it as a reminder that You have set me free. May I honor You as my Savior and Redeemer. Amen.

Find Rest as You Travel a Godly Path

This is what the LORD says: "Stop at the crossroads and look around. Ask for the old, godly way, and walk in it. Travel its path, and you will find rest for your souls."

JEREMIAH 6:16 NLT

———◆———

Lord, Your ways are tried and true. I know those who are old and gray now who have walked all of their lives with You. You have led them, and they have followed. May I live a godly life as these have done before me. May I now be the example for those who look to me as their guide. I will walk in Your ways and follow Your statues. I will find rest for my soul as I do so. Lord, You are good and Your love endures forever. Your mercies are new each morning. You sustain Your children and keep them in perfect peace. May I cling to the old rugged cross. May I walk in the ways of the righteous. May I find rest in doing so. In Jesus' name I pray, amen.

Make Me a Peacemaker

"God blesses those who work for peace,
for they will be called the children of God."

MATTHEW 5:9 NLT

Make me a peacemaker, Father. Day in and day out, make me a peacemaker. I admit that many times I am quick to argue my point. Give me wisdom, I pray. I need discernment to know when to remain quiet and when to speak up. Lord, may I look for and find opportunities tomorrow to work for peace. I want to be known as one who always seeks peace over strife. The world says to fight for what I want and to fight back when I am questioned or pushed. There are so many lawsuits today that the court schedules can't begin to keep up! May I seek always to sow peace in the world around me. Give me peace now and rest for my weary soul. In Jesus' name I ask, amen.

God of Comfort

Blessed be the God and Father of our
Lord Jesus Christ, the Father of
mercies and God of all comfort.

2 CORINTHIANS 1:3 NKJV

God of all comfort, meet me here tonight. I need to sense Your presence near and feel Your hand upon my weary brow. I need to be reminded that You are sovereign and in control. You have not taken Your hands off the wheel. You neither slumber nor sleep. I have known Your tender mercies in the past, and I so need to know them now. You are before all things and through You all things hold together. You are the Alpha and Omega, the beginning and the end. Nothing in my life comes as a shock to You. No setback or concern takes You by surprise. May I rest assured in that knowledge tonight. May I know again the strength found even in weakness, perhaps especially in weakness. Meet me here. Hold me close. I will draw upon Your comfort and Your peace through the night and into a new day. In Jesus' name I pray, amen.

Forgiving Others

Bearing with one another, and forgiving one another, if anyone has a complaint against another; even as Christ forgave you, so you also must do.

COLOSSIANS 3:13 NKJV

Lord, so often I find it hard to sleep at night. Whether it is finances or friendships, there is always something to worry about. I often lay awake thinking about forgiveness. I find it easy to forgive the little offenses, Father. But deep hurts reside within me and keep me awake at night. I want to forgive. I know that doing so will help me to move on and live a more peaceful life. But I find it impossible. Remind me tonight that I will never forgive others in my own strength. I must do it through Yours. I will never do it if I rely upon my sin nature. But I am a new creation, and You have given me a new nature and a new heart. As I have been greatly forgiven, may I also forgive greatly. In Jesus' name, amen.

Peace Found in God's Law

Great peace have those who love Your law,
and nothing causes them to stumble.

PSALM 119:165 NKJV

———◆———

Lord, tonight I ask You to renew my love for Your Word. I know that Your ways are the ways of life. I know that if I follow hard after You and meditate on Your Word, You will give me wisdom to make the best decisions. You will guide me on the right paths and keep my feet from slipping. Father, scripture is filled with promises that give me hope, and Your guidelines for my life give me pleasant boundaries. I often stray or just get lazy. I forget to read Your Word. I spend too many hours on social media or texting others. Help me lay down the phone and take up the Word of God. Give me great peace within its pages. May I follow it as my guidebook for life all of my days. Teach me even now as I open Your holy scriptures. In Jesus' name I pray, amen.

The Father's Discipline

No discipline seems pleasant at the time,
but painful. Later on, however, it produces
a harvest of righteousness and peace for
those who have been trained by it.

HEBREWS 12:11 NIV

Lord, like a child who is disciplined by his parent
for wandering into the street, I look up indignant
at first when You snatch me out of trouble. I
question You. I ask You why. I beg to be given
that which is not best for me. I want to step into
the forbidden territory. I want so badly to strike
off on my own. But later, I look back. I see the
why. I no longer question. I see Your hand of
mercy that at the time seemed to be keeping me
from my heart's desire. Father, help me to receive
Your discipline well. Help me to see it as it is. A
father disciplines the child he loves. Tonight, as I
close another day, I pray that if there is any area of
my life where You need to discipline me, I would
be aware. I would see it for what it is. I would
respond appropriately and respectfully. Amen.

Be Holy and Live at Peace with Others

Make every effort to live in peace with everyone and to be holy; without holiness no one will see the Lord.

HEBREWS 12:14 NIV

Lord, there are many words that could describe my actions and thoughts today. *Holy* might not be the first one that comes to mind! Each day it is a struggle, as I interact with those around me, to remember that You made every single one of them and I should live at peace with everyone. Remind me of this. Bring to mind this verse that speaks so strongly about holiness. I want to be one who is known as a peacemaker. I want to treat others with kindness and respect, even those with whom I disagree. Father, as I go to sleep tonight, bring to mind those I need to pray for. When I pray for others, my heart softens toward them and it's easier to live peacefully alongside them. Help each of my interactions tomorrow to be pleasing to you and make me a little more like Jesus each day. Make me holy, I pray, through the blood of Christ. Amen.

Pursuing Peace

Turn from evil and do good;
seek peace and pursue it.

PSALM 34:14 NIV

Lord, as light turns to darkness and another nighttime is upon me, I'm reminded of the dualities in Your Word. Light and dark. Good and evil. Life and death. Help me to seek Your truth always and turn from evil to good. Your ways are always higher. Your ways are always true. I think of how You pursue us, Lord. You pull us out of sin and clean us off and save us from the muck and mire of that life. You fill us up with abundance and goodness and grace. Just as You pursue me, Father, help me to pursue peace in every situation. Help me to represent my Abba Father well as I go into the world tomorrow. May my light shine for You. May my mouth speak of You. May my choices reflect You. May I rest well tonight in the shadow of Your wing, and may I pursue peace tomorrow. May it be at the forefront of my mind as I go into battle. May peace be my greatest weapon in the fight. In Jesus' name, amen.

Seeking Solitude

*But Jesus often withdrew to
lonely places and prayed.*
LUKE 5:16 NIV

Jesus, find me here. I am in a lonely place. I am
alone. I come before You and lay it all down. I
am found tonight as I will be in the end, alone.
Each of us will stand before Your throne of grace
and give an account, and my account will be Your
name. My reason for entrance into heaven will
be nothing but the blood of Jesus. And so, I come
before You now, just me. I do not hide in the
garden as Adam and Eve did. I call out to You to
meet me here, to find me even as I am, imperfect,
humbled before my King. I follow Your lead. I
withdraw at the close of my day. I end my day
in solitude. I seek You, for You tell me that when
I seek You with my whole heart, you will be
found. Be my whole heart. Be my guide. Be my
Lord, I ask. Give me peace as I close my eyes
and sleep. Give me strength for the new day
tomorrow. It is in Your name I pray, amen.

Mercy, Peace, and Love

To those who have been called, who are loved
in God the Father and kept for Jesus Christ:
Mercy, peace and love be yours in abundance.
JUDE 1:1–2 NIV

Lord, forgive me for the sins I committed today.
I pause now and admit them to You. I made
choices that did not honor You, and I need Your
merciful forgiveness. I come before You in need
of love. I feel a little less loved when I do wrong.
I think it is my humanity that makes this so.
I am used to conditional love, not the unconditional type You pour out so freely. Help me
to feel Your arms around me. Help me to rest
in a love that will never let me go, no matter
what. I ask You tonight, perhaps above all, for
peace. You promise me peace that the world
cannot give. You offer it so freely, and yet I trade
that beautiful peace for worry and strife. Touch
my weary brow and fill me tonight with peace
that passes all understanding. May mercy, peace,
and love be mine in abundance because I am a
child of the living God, the King of kings, the
mighty One who saves. In Jesus' name, amen.

Making Time for Rest

*But so many people were coming and going that
Jesus and the apostles did not even have a chance
to eat. Then Jesus said, "Let's go to a place where
we can be alone and get some rest." They left in
a boat for a place where they could be alone.*

MARK 6:31–32 CEV

Jesus, You made time for rest when You walked
this earth. You called Your disciples away from
work to be alone with You, to eat and rest. You
saw value in that. You reminded the twelve, in
the midst of service, that solace was high on
Your list as well. As I close this day, with all the
demands it brought, I rest in You. This day may
not have held the famous feeding of the five
thousand as that one did, and my feet do not
step in the prints left by Your sandals on the
shore. But You are with me, Savior, just as real
as You were there with them. And You call me
to this quiet place where just the two of us can
commune. What a sweet, sweet Savior I serve.
Thank You for calling me to rest. Amen.

Peace in the Midst of Suffering

I have told you this, so that you might have peace in your hearts because of me. While you are in the world, you will have to suffer. But cheer up! I have defeated the world.

JOHN 16:33 CEV

———•———

Lord, I am often overwhelmed by all those who are sick and lost and in need. I find myself wondering sometimes how the world can get any darker. Cancer. Addictions. Brokenness. Divorce. Bullying. The suffering goes on. I see it in the faces of those who pass me on the street. I see it on social media. It is all over the nightly news. God, why should I be surprised? You told us it would be this way. This world is full of suffering. The good news is that You have overcome this world. You are above and beyond it all. One day there will be no more suffering and no more sorrow. For now, I rejoice in You and rest in the hope that I have as a believer. Bring a cheerfulness over me that I might shine as a light for you in this hurting world. Even though there is suffering, there is Jesus! And He is so much more! Amen.

Peace

Don't worry about anything, but pray about
everything. With thankful hearts offer up your
prayers and requests to God. Then, because you
belong to Christ Jesus, God will bless you with
peace that no one can completely understand. And
this peace will control the way you think and feel.

PHILIPPIANS 4:6–7 CEV

Lord Jesus, take my worries. Hear my prayers.
With a thankful heart, I present my requests
before You. Because I am Yours, I am blessed
with a deep peace. It is a peace that, although
I try, I cannot explain. Words cannot do it jus-
tice. It is not comprehended by the world. But
when I speak of it to another believer, particu-
larly one who has lived awhile in this world
with its sorrows, I see a sparkle of recognition.
She knows that peace too. She nods. She smiles.
What a gift to be the recipient of a peace like
that. A peace that controls my mind and my
heart. A peace that allows me to rest my head
on my pillow tonight, knowing that You are still
in control. Thank You for peace that passes all
understanding. Amen.

Trading Burdens for Peace

Therefore humble yourselves under the
mighty hand of God, that He may exalt
you at the proper time, casting all your
anxiety on Him, because He cares for you.
1 PETER 5:6–7 NASB

Mighty God, I come before You. I humble myself. You are Creator, and I am the created. You will lift me up at the right time. You are before all things. You hold all things together. You are my God. I put my trust in You. I quiet myself before You now, after the busy chaos of the day. I cast my anxiety before You, holding nothing back. I express it to You in the way that You made me to, a little different I suppose from every other person. I cry. I speak. I tell You the worries that You already know are weighing me down. And as I do, they feel lighter. You tell me to give You my burdens and to find my rest in You. What a gift this is, the unloading of a pack that has left its mark on me. Take my weariness now and replace it with peace. Thank You for Your abiding care for me. Amen.

The Lord Is Near

The Lord is near to the brokenhearted and
saves those who are crushed in spirit.

PSALM 34:18 NASB

───────◆───────

Lord, I am brokenhearted. You find me crushed
in spirit and bind my wounds. You start in on
the work of filling in the gaps. And when I feel
as if I just can't go on, I do. Not as the result of
a catchy "keep fighting" slogan or a 5K cause.
Not because of some strength I muster up on
my own. But because of Jesus. A baby born in
a stable on a dark night in Bethlehem so many
years ago. A sinless Savior, a carpenter King
whose nail-scarred hands reach out to me again
and again and again. The pieces of my heart are
stronger as You put them back together, adding
wisdom and peace. You are near. I rest in that
nearness. I thank You for knitting me together
in my mother's womb and for putting my heart
back together a million times over in this life.
You find me crushed but set me on the path
again whole. Amen.

Trust in the Lord

When I am afraid, I will put my trust in You.
PSALM 56:3 NASB

Lord, the night brings fears. Children ask their parents to check their closets and under their beds for monsters. Such a simple fix is not helpful to adults, but I have found the answer. I put my trust in You. In the darkness, I remember what You have shown me in the light. The darkness of the night, and the evil of this world, will not frighten me. I am a daughter of the King of kings. I am a child of God. I rest in that tonight. I bask in the knowledge that nothing can snatch me from Your hand. Nothing can steal my peace. Whatever this life may bring, I am ready—because I have You. Thank You for being near. Thank You for loving me with an unfailing love. Thank You for understanding the frailness of my human heart and the fears that overwhelm. I trust You with my worries. I lay them down at Your feet as I lay my body down to rest. Tuck me in tonight and wrap me up in the blanket of Your sovereign security. In Jesus' name I pray, amen.

Ending the Day

Finally, brothers and sisters, whatever is true, whatever is noble, whatever is right, whatever is pure, whatever is lovely, whatever is admirable— if anything is excellent or praiseworthy—think about such things. Whatever you have learned or received or heard from me, or seen in me—put it into practice. And the God of peace will be with you.

PHILIPPIANS 4:8–9 NIV

God, I will dwell upon what is true. As I end this day, I will focus not on the wrong but the right. I will bask in that which is noble. I will gaze upon that which is admirable. I will look for the lovely. I will think on Your teachings. I will remember how You lived on this earth. I will pour out grace like confetti, celebrating the freedom to do so because I am a recipient of it. I will know the peace of God because I know the God of peace. I will rest. I will sleep. I will let this day slip away and tomorrow, where I failed today, I will do better. Tomorrow brings promise. The promise of a redo. The promise of a second chance. Thank You for that, Father. In Jesus' name I pray, amen.

Draw Near

Draw near to God and He
will draw near to you.
JAMES 4:8 NASB

Lord, I draw near to You tonight. I love that You promise me in Your Word when I do so, You will draw near to me. That's all it takes. Drawing near. Turning from the day's demands to my Lord's love. Resting in You. Remember who I am and whose I am. Lord, thank You for the comfort I find in Your arms. Thank you for washing a peace over my soul regardless of the fact that tomorrow will bring some of the same challenges that today brought. In this world there is trouble. You said it would be so. But You have overcome the world. And through You, Christ Jesus, I am more than a conqueror. Come near to me now. As a child in her mother's arms, I rest against Your strong chest and I can almost hear Your heartbeat. It beats for Your world, Your creation, Your children. Thank You, Lord, for being here. For being a God who draws near. Amen.

Even While I Sleep

God takes care of his own,
even while they sleep.
PSALM 127:2 CEV

God, You take care of me—even while I sleep.
You never slumber. You are always watching over
me. As a child, I drifted off to sleep peacefully
because I heard my parents' voices in the next
room. I saw that sliver of light under the door
that said someone in the house was still up. Someone was on guard. Like a mother slipping into
the nursery time and time again throughout
the night, just to be sure all is well, You are my
constant watch keeper. You sing over me. You
touch my brow. You smile upon me. Imperfect
as I am, and as many times as I go astray or let
You down, You are my Father and You love me
with a God love. A love that is not of this world.
A love that never goes away, never leaves, never
lets go, never turns the light off, never shuts the
door. You cover me with Your affections. You
take care of me while I sleep. Thank You for
that, Father. What a sweet, sweet Father You
are. Amen.

God Is My Protector

*The Lord is your protector, and he won't
go to sleep or let you stumble. The protector
of Israel doesn't doze or ever get drowsy.*

PSALM 121:3–4 CEV

Father, You are my Protector. You never sleep or slumber. You don't even get drowsy. What a protector I have in You! Thank You for looking out for me all day and all night. I have nothing to fear. I give You my concerns and my questions tonight. I give You the worries of the day. I ask that You clear my mind and give me rest that I might be ready to face a new day. Each day has enough trouble of its own. Help me never to be a borrower of trouble. When anxiety sneaks in, I pray You will stop it in its tracks. You are my Protector, and I will trust in You. Just as the children's prayer says: "Now I lay me down to sleep, I pray the Lord my soul to keep." In Jesus' name I pray, amen.

One Day at a Time

Don't worry about tomorrow. It will take care
of itself. You have enough to worry about today.
MATTHEW 6:34 CEV

———————

Lord, I do not want to be a borrower of trouble.
You tell me in Your Word that each day will take
care of itself. Sometimes I struggle with looking
too far into the future. Help me, God, to rely
on the promises of the Bible. They are tried and
true. They come straight from Your heart of provision and love for me. When I read in Jeremiah
that You know the plans You have for me, let that
truth resonate with my spirit. Cause me to rest
in the assurance that You have plans to prosper
me and not to harm me. You always have my best
interest at heart. I have a limited perspective. In
my humanness, I see only one piece of the puzzle
at a time. You see the completed puzzle. You are
standing back and admiring the finished product
while I am wringing my hands when one piece
doesn't seem to fit. Bring me rest now, I pray,
and allow me to release all the worries of this day
to You. In Jesus' name I ask, amen.

A Wonderful Offer

If you are tired from carrying heavy burdens, come
to me and I will give you rest. Take the yoke I give
you. Put it on your shoulders and learn from me.
I am gentle and humble, and you will find rest.

MATTHEW 11:28–29 CEV

Jesus, what a wonderful offer I find in the book of Matthew! You offer a trade I cannot resist. You will take my heavy burdens and replace them with rest. The stress of my day you will replace with your gentleness. Gentleness sounds really good right now! Help me to learn from You. Help me to follow Your lead. You did not worry and toil during your earthly ministry. You did not even have a home to call Your own, and yet, You were not filled with anxiety. You asked the Father, and He provided for You. You met needs. You served. But You also rested. You ate. I imagine You laughed with those disciples in Your inner circle! Thank You for this marvelous offer to lift this heavy backpack of burdens off my shoulders. Help me to receive it thankfully. Give me rest from my busy day. In Jesus' name, amen.

Be Still and Know

"Be still, and know that I am God! I will
be honored by every nation. I will be
honored throughout the world."

PSALM 46:10 NLT

Sweet Father, You tell me to be still. And so I am.
In these moments, as I close my eyes and close the
day, I choose to be silent and at rest before You.
I breathe You in deep as I exhale the stressors of
the day. I invite You into this moment so that I
may know and feel and experience who You are.
You are God, above all things, holding all things
together, including this life I lead day by day.
Thank You for being there and for being God.
You are the same yesterday, today, and tomorrow.
In my ever-changing world, this constant brings
great peace. Thank You for telling me in Your
Word that in order to really know my God, I must
be still. It is hard to hear Your still, small voice
when I am surrounded by noise. Thank You for
these tranquil nighttime moments I spend with
You. Meet me here. Be honored in my stillness,
I pray. Amen.

Refuge and Strength

God is our refuge and strength,
always ready to help in times of trouble.

PSALM 46:1 NLT

———————

Heavenly Father, You stand ready to help. You are my Refuge. You assure me I can run to You at any time. Like a child hiding in a parent's embrace, I lose myself in Your protection. I rest in Your sovereignty. I trust in Your omniscience. You are my Strength. When I am weakest, You meet me. You are strong. In You, I can take on the next day, or hour, or moment. I can face the decisions that must be made. I can run the household. I can raise the child. I can fulfill the duties of the job. I can end the dysfunctional relationship. I can stoke the fires of the marriage that have burned out. I can smile in the face of crisis. I can do the hard thing and do it well. Because my hope is found in You, and because You are strong, I am strong as well. Thank You for being my Refuge and my Strength. I never have to wonder where to turn for help. I turn to You. You are my Help. Goodnight, God. I love You. Amen.

A Heart Ruled by Peace

And let the peace that comes from Christ rule in your hearts. For as members of one body you are called to live in peace. And always be thankful.

COLOSSIANS 3:15 NLT

Christ Jesus, may peace rule in my heart tonight. May it reign, subduing chaos, chasing down anxiety and stamping it out. I imagine a kingdom ruled by peace—with a king whose scepter is patience and whose army bears harmony and tranquility as its weapons. May my heart be such a haven. May I find rest in You for, as You spoke from the cross that dark day, *"It is finished."* You did not leave work for me. You completed the last task and crossed it off the list. You did not build a partial bridge. It spans the chasm between a holy God and little sinful me absolutely perfectly. All I need do is take Your hand and cross over. And so tonight I lay my worries down. I relinquish sorrow. I drop my tight hold on perfectionism and works. I reach out and accept the gift of peace. May it rule in me and over me all the days of my life. Amen.

I am Fully Known

*You saw me before I was born. Every day of my
life was recorded in your book. Every moment
was laid out before a single day had passed.*

PSALM 139:16 NLT

God, You know me so well. You have every day of
my life recorded in Your book—the ones I have
already lived and the ones that are yet to come.
I find comfort in that tonight as I lie down to
rest. Before I even started this crazy race called
life, You were standing at the finish line. You
see the beautiful tapestry, the completed puzzle, the final product. To think that I was Your
idea! Your Word says that You knit me together in
my mother's womb. Whether my parents planned
me or not, You did! Whether they wanted me or
not, You did! Whether the road has been bumpy
or smooth to get me to this place, You have been
there all along. And You will never leave me.
What a promise! What a comfort! Thank You
for having such a deep, complete knowledge of
me, Lord. Help me to rest in You now. Bear with
me, I ask, as I learn to trust in You as my Abba
Father, my Daddy. Amen.

God Is Greater Than Darkness

I could ask the darkness to hide me and the light around me to become night—but even in darkness I cannot hide from you. To you the night shines as bright as day. Darkness and light are the same to you.

PSALM 139:11–12 NLT

God, even the darkness cannot hide me from You. You are greater than the darkness. Just as a candle dispels the blackness of the night, Your light overtakes and fills the rooms of our souls. Darkness has no power over You. As mere humans, we are limited by darkness. Our work typically takes place in the daytime. When the sun sets, we go to our homes. We end our day. We rest. The darkness sends us packing. But You know no limits. You are not bound by hours on the clock or the shadows of the night. Find me here, Father. Chase away my fears. May Your presence bring me comfort. Wrap me up in the blanket of Your power and might. Touch my weary brow with peace. In Jesus' name I pray, amen.

My Help Comes from the Lord

You satisfy me more than the richest feast.
I will praise you with songs of joy. I lie awake
thinking of you, meditating on you through the
night. Because you are my helper, I sing for joy
in the shadow of your wings. I cling to you;
your strong right hand holds me securely.
PSALM 63:5–8 NLT

Satisfier of my soul, I come to You tonight. I praise You as I recall all the times You have shown up to help me in the past. When I wake up anxious in the night, bring to mind all the help You have provided through the years. You never leave me hanging. How amazing to know that You hold me with Your strong right hand! Like a little child who is carried high upon her daddy's shoulders am I, a daughter of the King! You lift me up, high above the toil and trouble of this world. You are my Help. I need look nowhere else. All I have to do is call on You, Father. Thank You for being my Help at all times, in all ways, on all of my days. Amen.

Lifter of My Head

But you, Lord, are a shield around me, my glory,
the One who lifts my head high. I call out to the
Lord, and he answers me from his holy mountain.
PSALM 3:3–4 NIV

———————— ••• ————————

Lord, You are the lifter of my head. You are my shield of protection. You answer when I call. What promises of comfort and care I find in this one verse of scripture! When the world beats me up and tears me down, You are there. You touch my chin. You tilt my weary head back and hold it in Your hands. You lift my heart as You lift my head. You encourage me. You remind me as the sun goes down on another day exactly who I belong to. I am Yours. I am found in You. My identity is not defined by what people say about me. You declare me righteous through the blood of Christ shed for me upon the cross of Calvary. Surround me now with Your protection. Thank You for hearing my prayers. You are never too far to come running when I call to You. I love You, Lord. Amen.

The Blessing of Sleep

The sleep of a laborer is sweet, whether
they eat little or much, but as for the rich,
their abundance permits them no sleep.

ECCLESIASTES 5:12 NIV

God, thank You for the promise of sweet sleep.
When my day's work is done, rest is a great reward. Whether I work in my home or outside of
it, my day holds a to-do list a mile long. Sometimes I feel guilty when I put down the work
and rest. Help me to remember how greatly You
value sleep and rest. You rested when You walked
on earth. You drew away to quiet places with
Your disciples, those closest to You. You stole
away alone as well. You met with the Father. You
slept. You were even known to sleep through a
raging storm when the disciples were afraid. There
was nothing to fear. Their Savior slept. Wow. If
You value sleep, so do I. I quiet myself before
You now. I am still that I might know that You
are God. I close my eyes and accept the gift of
sweet sleep. I love You, Lord. Amen.

Sweet Sleep

*In vain you rise early and stay up late, toiling for
food to eat—for he grants sleep to those he loves.*

PSALM 127:2 NIV

———————

Heavenly Father, thank You for rest. Thank You
that I need not scurry about toiling for my needs.
There is no need to rise before it is time to do
so. There is no need to stay up all hours of the
night! Certainly, there is work to be done. But at
the end of the day, You call me to lay the work
down. You grant me peaceful sleep. Thank You
for that. I need it so! I awake so fully refreshed
after a peaceful rest, ready to take on the next
day. When I don't rest, no one benefits. I am not
nearly as productive on such days. Certainly those
under my guidance or those for whom I provide
care suffer when I lack sleep. Provide that sweet
peace promised to Your children in Psalms. Bring
a calm over me that the world cannot compre-
hend, a peace that passes all understanding. Thank
You for rest. In Jesus' name, amen.

Trusting That Jesus Is in Control

Jesus was in the stern, sleeping on a cushion.
The disciples woke him and said to him,
"Teacher, don't you care if we drown?"

MARK 4:38 NIV

———————————

Jesus, so often I second-guess You, don't I? Like the disciples who woke You up during the storm and questioned Your care for them, I doubt You. Teach me, Lord, that with You there is a right time for everything. You never act before it is time, and You are never too late. You are always right on schedule. You see my need, and You meet it in just the right way, at just the right time. The disciples were shocked to see You sleeping, and yet, You had everything under control. That storm was no match for their Savior! Give me a peace that whispers calm over me—even in the midst of the strongest tempest. May I be marked with the serenity of a Christ follower. May I trust in You more each day. As I lie down and go to sleep, I rest in You, Jesus. Amen.

God Sings over Me

"The Lord your God is with you, the Mighty Warrior who saves. He will take great delight in you; in his love he will no longer rebuke you, but will rejoice over you with singing."

ZEPHANIAH 3:17 NIV

———❦———

Lord, my God, You are, as the scripture states, the Mighty Warrior who saves. You take delight in me. I am Your child. You rejoice over me with singing. Just as a family gathers and "oohs and aahs" over a newborn baby, You find great joy in simply being my Father. You do not love me because of my works, but often in spite of them. You love me just as much on my worst days as my best ones. You desire to be with me when I have let You down just as much as when I have represented You well. Your love is not conditional. It is a free gift. It is not earned, but it must be accepted, like a present. I reach out to You. I accept Your love. I listen to the songs You sing over me. I relish these moments as I drift off to sleep. I am a daughter of the King. Your lullabies bring me great comfort. Amen.

A Thankful Heart

*Give thanks in all circumstances; for this
is God's will for you in Christ Jesus.*

1 THESSALONIANS 5:18 NIV

God, it is Your will that I give thanks in all circumstances. Scripture does not call me to gratefulness only on days that go smooth from start to finish. It does not direct me to be thankful when it's easy. It says to be thankful in *all* circumstances. That includes today! As I reflect on the happenings of my day, not all of them left me feeling thankful. Remind me that it is not about feelings. Thankfulness is a choice. It is a decision. It is a way of life and a mind-set. It is looking for the light and the lovely rather than dwelling on the dark and dismal. I choose thankfulness. As I close this day, I list before you three things for which I am grateful. This list will look different each day it is composed. Give me the discipline that it takes to be thankful and positive in a world that so easily pulls me down and encourages me to complain and live in negativity. In Jesus' name I ask, amen.

Secure in the Lord

My heart is not proud, Lord, my eyes are not
haughty; I do not concern myself with great
matters or things too wonderful for me. But I
have calmed and quieted myself, I am like a
weaned child with its mother; like a weaned
child I am content. Israel, put your hope in
the Lord both now and forevermore.

PSALM 131:1–3 NIV

———◆———

Lord, thank You for the calm and quiet that I
find in You. You are my haven, my quiet place,
my home. I don't have to be concerned with the
future or with matters outside of my control. I
need not toss and turn with anxiety in the night.
You are sovereign. You see all. You know all. You
have never let things spin out of control, and You
are not about to start now. Thank You for the
sense of security I feel as I close my eyes tonight.
I am secure in You. Like a child trusts her parent,
I trust in You, oh Lord. In Jesus' name, amen.

More Like Jesus

A hot-tempered person stirs up conflict,
but the one who is patient calms a quarrel.

PROVERBS 15:18 NIV

God, I come to You tonight, recognizing that
sometimes I blend in with the world around
me a bit too well. As a Christian, I should stand
out as different. I should be a bit conspicuous in
the crowd because my attitudes and actions go
against the flow. Your Word tells me that the one
who is patient calms a quarrel. Help me to be
the one. The one who is more patient than would
be expected under the circumstances. The one
who is more compassionate and takes time to
meet a need. The one who is more caring and
stops to listen. Work even now in my mind and
heart, even as I sleep through the night. Trans-
form me so that, day by day, I look a little more
like Christ. Make me the one, I pray. Amen.

Calm in the Storm

*He got up, rebuked the wind and said to the
waves, "Quiet! Be still!" Then the wind
died down and it was completely calm.*

MARK 4:39 NIV

Jesus, just as You calmed the storm, You calm
my spirit within me. I don't know how people
survive the trials and tribulations of life without
You at their side. You, my Savior, bring a peace
over me. I hear people talk about their "person."
You are my "person." You are the first one I turn
to when I feel alone. You find me when I am
lost. You show me the way when I am confused.
When I am insecure, You remind me that my
identity is in You and in You alone. What the
world says about me is not important. I have
an audience of One. Thank You for being
the calming force in my life. Thank You for rest
and for the sleep that lies ahead of me tonight.
I love You, Lord. Amen.

Holy Spirit

"And I will ask the Father, and he will give
you another advocate to help you and be with
you forever—the Spirit of truth. The world
cannot accept him, because it neither sees him
nor knows him. But you know him, for he lives
with you and will be in you. I will not leave
you as orphans; I will come to you."

JOHN 14:16–18 NIV

Heavenly Father, thank You for sending the Holy
Spirit. My Helper and Advocate, the Spirit of
truth. A Comforter and Counselor. He lives
within me. He guides and directs me. He shows
me right from wrong. He came. He showed up.
When You took Jesus back to heaven with You,
You sent us the gift of the Holy Ghost. And
what a gift He is in my life! So many times I
think of something at just the right time. I feel
led to pray for someone. I am nudged toward an
act of kindness. I feel guided in a certain direction or calmed in the midst of confusion. It is
then that I look up. I whisper a prayer. I thank
You for the Holy Spirit and the huge difference
He makes in my life. Amen.

Prayer

In the same way, the Spirit helps us in our
weakness. We do not know what we ought
to pray for, but the Spirit himself intercedes
for us through wordless groans.

ROMANS 8:26 NIV

God in heaven, and right here with me now, the
mystery of prayer baffles me. That I am allowed
to commune with the Creator astounds me. I
fellowship with the Father when I am but a sinful
woman here on earth. Thank You for providing
a way that I may come before You. I start each
day talking with You. I close each day in the
same manner. Hear my prayers, Lord. Hear me
as I pour out my heart before You. I praise You,
thank You, and I cry out to You to meet needs
in my own life and in the lives of those I love.
And when there are no words, I trust that the
Spirit intercedes for me. Sometimes the hurt is
too deep, the need too great. I just say, "Jesus." I
just call upon the Way, the Truth, and the Life,
and I let the Spirit do the rest of the work of
prayer. I love You, Lord, and I love the beautiful
privilege of prayer. Amen.

God Created Rest

By the seventh day God completed His work
which He had done, and He rested on the
seventh day from all His work which He had
done. Then God blessed the seventh day and
sanctified it, because in it He rested from all
His work which God had created and made.

GENESIS 2:2–3 NASB

Father, we get so caught up in work. It is the American way, I suppose. A term has even been created to capture it—*workaholic*. We shake our heads in disapproval at drug or alcohol addicts, and yet, we burn the candle at both ends far too many days. We neglect things that matter just to keep working. We give work far too many hours of each day and often work into the night. Remind me, Father, that while certainly work was Your idea, You also created rest. You deemed it good. You blessed and sanctified it. You called it right. You did it Yourself. Give me rest now, I pray. Make it plentiful and peaceful. I need it so. Thank You for rest. Help me to value it just as much as I value work. May it be a priority in my life, I ask in Jesus' name. Amen.

God Is with Me

And He said, "My presence shall go
with you, and I will give you rest."

EXODUS 33:14 NASB

———— ◆ ————

Father, just like Moses, I do not want to go unless You lead me. You change everything. Your presence brings power. You take my hand in Yours. You lift my head. You don't leave my side. You promised to give Moses and the Israelites rest on their journey. I find my rest in You as well. As You go before me, paving the way, I will follow You into tomorrow even though I don't know what it holds. Because You go with me, I am able to face the unknown. I rest in the knowledge that I am never alone. On my darkest day, in the deepest valley, I walk with the Lord Almighty. May the trumpets sound as the walls of my trials come tumbling down! May the waters part before me at just the moment I need to pass through! You are God and You are mighty and powerful. And yet, Your presence goes with me. Thank You that I am never alone. Amen.

Good Shepherd

The Lord is my shepherd, I shall not want.
He makes me lie down in green pastures;
He leads me beside quiet waters. He restores
my soul; He guides me in the paths of
righteousness for His name's sake.

PSALM 23:1–3 NASB

Lord, You are the Good Shepherd. I have no need You can't meet. You lead me to quiet waters. I drink deep and am refreshed. You show me places of rest throughout my day. You point out moments I can grab for prayer in spite of deadlines and duties. You sort through all the paths that lie before us, and You guide me to the right ones. All I have to do is ask. I simply look up into my Shepherd's compassionate eyes. You want nothing but good for me. I am Yours, and You take that ownership so seriously. If I get lost from the fold, You come after me. You don't just wish me well. You come after me. Thank You, Lord, for being all I need. Through the dull roar of the world around me, I hear Your still, small voice. I know the voice of my Shepherd, and it is life changing. In Jesus' name, amen.

No Fear

*Even though I walk through the valley
of the shadow of death, I fear no evil, for You
are with me; Your rod and Your staff, they
comfort me. You prepare a table before me
in the presence of my enemies; You have
anointed my head with oil; my cup overflows.*

PSALM 23:4–5 NASB

Lord, thank You that I never have to fear. Not
when the pressure is over the top or the bottom
falls out. Not when the pink slip comes, or the
divorce papers. Not when the doctor's report
bears the C word, and the treatment plan seems
unbearable. Not ever. Not even when the end
draws near. Because You are with me. You protect
me. You direct me. You meet my needs. You heal
me. You bless me beyond measure. You hold on
to me. You know me, and You never let go. I walk
with You on the good days and the bad alike. I
resist the urge to run ahead or lag behind. I find
my pace moving at Your side. I set my rhythm as
I fall in step with You. Good Shepherd, Jehovah-
jireh, almighty God, I will walk with You. Amen.

Creator God

When I consider Your heavens, the work of Your fingers, the moon and the stars, which You have ordained; what is man that You take thought of him, and the son of man that You care for him?

PSALM 8:3–4 NASB

God in heaven and right here with me now, the moon in all its glory shines tonight. Like a bright orange fireball in the sky, it blazes for all to see. It is a symbol to me of Your magnificent creation. It hangs in the sky so far from me, and yet shines so brightly it feels as if I could reach out and touch it. Your creation is amazing. It speaks of the master designer who put each tree in its place and causes each flower to bloom. As I end this day and thank You for caring for me so well, I thank You also for the beauty of Your world. I am so blessed to enjoy the creation and to know the Creator as Father and friend. In Jesus' name I pray, amen.

Rock and Redeemer

Let the words of my mouth and the meditation
of my heart be acceptable in Your sight,
O Lord, my rock and my Redeemer.

PSALM 19:14 NASB

———◆———

Heavenly Father, thank You for this day. Thank You for walking with me each step of the way. Today brought joys and sorrows. It was filled with little victories and little pitfalls. Life is a mix of ups and downs, smiles and frowns. As I go to bed tonight, may my focus be solely upon You. May I leave the cares of the day and the concerns of tomorrow at Your feet. May my prayer and even my meditation be pleasing to You. May it be acceptable to a holy God I am so blessed to converse with. You are my Rock, Lord. I have such a firm foundation for my life because I am Your child. I turn to You and You are always there. You are my Redeemer, Lord. You have brought beauty from ashes in this little life. I still myself before You now. Be honored in my prayer. Be honored in my silence. Amen.

My God

"I will give them hearts that recognize me as the LORD. They will be my people, and I will be their God, for they will return to me wholeheartedly."

JEREMIAH 24:7 NLT

———•———

Oh Lord my God, give me a clean heart. Purify my thoughts and feelings. Help me to remember that You are my God and I am Your child. You have chosen me from the beginning of time. You have ordained me as Your own and marked each of my days as blessed. I am never alone, never wandering, never forsaken. I always have my God. I always have You on my side. When I consider all the paths my heart has taken, some desolate and disappointing, I realize that every time I turn right back to You. You take me back into Your arms. You welcome me, for I am not a stranger to You. I am known fully and yet loved completely by You. I am Yours and, praise Jesus, You are mine. Hold me tight, heavenly Father. Remind me tonight that You are my God. May I always return to You wholeheartedly. Amen.

Focusing on Him

You will keep in perfect peace all who trust in you,
all whose thoughts are fixed on you!
ISAIAH 26:3 NLT

Sweet Jesus, I come before You now, tired. Exhausted really. The sun has set on yet another day. I have given it my best. My best doesn't seem like enough. When I go to bed, I bring with me thoughts of the ways I failed today and thoughts of how others failed me. It is hard to shake work pressure and family stresses. It is difficult to close my eyes and unload the weight of the world I carry. But Your Word says if I will fix my thoughts on You, You will keep me in perfect peace. This is Your promise to all who trust in You. Show me, Savior, how to focus my mind on You. Rid me of worry. In these moments spent with You before bed, cause me to just rest in You. You are strong enough and big enough to take my load for me. I want to fix my thoughts on You alone. Amen.

Laying Down My Phone

*They do not fear bad news; they confidently
trust the Lord to care for them.*

PSALM 112:7 NLT

Lord, there are nights when I go to bed but
anxiety causes me to check my phone a few
more times before I drift off to sleep. The next
morning it is the first thing I do. Is there a text?
A voice mail? Did I get that call or that email?
Cause me to let that go a little, Father. I need
not worry that I will miss something. You have
everything under control. You have children and
parents and colleagues in Your care. You never
sleep or slumber. And I never need to fear bad
news. Even the disappointments, breakups, negative medical tests, and losses are manageable
for You. You are sovereign and above all things.
Help me to confidently trust in You and to lay
down the phone for a while in order to spend time
with my Lord and go to sleep in peace. Amen.

Worship through Song

My heart is confident in you, O God; my heart is
confident. No wonder I can sing your praises!
PSALM 57:7 NLT

Father, I praise You. I praise You in the morning,
and I praise You now as I prepare for a good night's
sleep. I lift up my song to You as I end this day.
Whether my song is a hymn tried and true or a
contemporary chorus, I will bring You my best. I
give You my songs as an offering. I lift You up! My
heart swells with joy and thanksgiving that I am
loved by my heavenly Father. My mind is at rest.
My soul gives way to worship. My song declares
Your glory. May You be lifted high. May You be
honored now through my song, and may You
go with me through this night and into another
day if it is Your will that the sun shall rise again.
I love You, Lord. Thank You for music. It is such
an amazing way to praise You, my beloved. In
Jesus' name I pray, amen.

Focusing on the Lord

*Behold, as the eyes of servants look to the
hand of their master, as the eyes of a maid to
the hand of her mistress, so our eyes look to
the Lord our God, until He is gracious to us.*

PSALM 123:2 NASB

Lord, there are so many distractions that fill each
day and night. Electronics, TV, social media, cell
phones. They dominate the American life. Give
me wisdom as I meditate before You tonight.
Show me where I can rid myself of some of
these distractions. Teach me how to look to You
with the same focus that a servant watches her
master. I don't want to come to heaven's gates
and discover a list of missed opportunities to
worship and serve You because I was caught up in
lesser things. I want my life to shine as a light in
this dark world. I want to be known as one who
follows hard after You, Lord. Show me what I
need to do even if it seems extreme in my culture.
If it means pulling the plug on the television or
canceling a social media account, give me the
strength to walk away from the distraction in
order to focus solely on You. Amen.

Focus on the Future

Brethren, I do not regard myself as having laid hold of it yet; but one thing I do: forgetting what lies behind and reaching forward to what lies ahead, I press on toward the goal for the prize of the upward call of God in Christ Jesus.

PHILIPPIANS 3:13–14 NASB

———

Heavenly Father, thank You that each day I get a do-over. You present me with a clean slate and a fresh start. You encourage me to forget the past and press on toward the finish line. I have an upward call. I am not called to dwell in the past where regret bogs me down. I am drawn and pushed and carried forward by my forgiving, future-driven Father. You have plans for me, plans to bring me hope, plans to use me and to bless me. May I release to You this day whatever it brought, whatever it held for me. And as I do, there is space made in my life and I eagerly look forward to tomorrow morning when my new day begins. May it be a day in which I honor and walk closely with You, my Lord. Amen.

Seeking Him

Therefore if you have been raised up with Christ,
keep seeking the things above, where Christ is,
seated at the right hand of God.

COLOSSIANS 3:1 NASB

———————

Christ Jesus, You are seated at the right hand of God. You are heaven's glory, the Son of God, the Savior of the world, my Redeemer and friend. You are worthy of all praise. I worship You as daylight gives way to darkness tonight. Thank You for raising me up. Thank You for seeing my need and meeting it. You were the only one who could right my wrongs. You were the only payment for sin. You were the only bridge builder, and You took that job so seriously that it cost You Your life. There are no words for such a sacrifice. And so, in my awe and in my thanksgiving, I choose to seek each day the things that are above. Prepare me even now for a new day tomorrow, another day to seek You with my whole heart. Amen.

Run the Race

*Therefore, since we have so great a cloud
of witnesses surrounding us, let us also lay
aside every encumbrance and the sin which
so easily entangles us, and let us run with
endurance the race that is set before us, fixing
our eyes on Jesus, the author and perfecter of
faith, who for the joy set before Him endured
the cross, despising the shame, and has sat
down at the right hand of the throne of God.*

HEBREWS 12:1–2 NASB

Lord, I turn my eyes upon You. You are the beginning and the end. You are the object of my faith. Without You, there is no hope for tomorrow. But with You, there is every hope! Bring to mind as I pray tonight the sins that I need to confess and repent from. Sin drags me down. It keeps me from You. It is always ready to catch me in its trap. Protect my heart and mind. I choose to lay aside sin and run hard after You, Christ Jesus. This race is not for the faint of heart. It takes daily surrender, and I choose to keep fighting, keep running, keep surrendering. I run for my King. Amen.

Not to the Left or Right

*Keep vigilant watch over your heart; that's
where life starts. Don't talk out of both sides
of your mouth; avoid careless banter, white lies,
and gossip. Keep your eyes straight ahead; ignore
all sideshow distractions. Watch your step, and
the road will stretch out smooth before you. Look
neither right nor left; leave evil in the dust.*

PROVERBS 4:25–27 MSG

God, the distractions of this world call to me.
They beg for my attention. It is so easy to fall
in step with the world, but I know I am called
to be set apart. I am but an alien here on this
earth. My real home is heaven. My identity is not
found in social media likes or comments. My
worth is not determined by fashion or how amazing and unique the birthday party I give for my
child is. My hope is found in Christ alone. I say
that, and yet I need so much help, Lord, to live
it out day by day. As I rest before You now, reju-
venate my spirit. Prepare me for battle tomorrow.
I want to stay on track with You, not swayed to
the left or the right. Amen.

God Hears

*"When my life was ebbing away,
I remembered you, Lord, and my
prayer rose to you, to your holy temple."*

JONAH 2:7 NIV

———————•———————

God, Jonah prayed to You from the belly of the big fish. His prayer got through to You! When I find myself feeling as if I have reached the end of my rope, remind me of this amazing story of Your faithfulness. Even though Your servant had gone astray, You were there. You rescued him from the pit. You lifted him up. You used him again. And he was made new. He carried out Your commands and followed Your lead. He did not make the same mistake again. Nineveh seemed impossible to him, but he went. He knew what it was like to hit rock bottom. He remembered that time in the whale's belly, didn't he? Give me the confidence of Jonah as I make my prayer before You tonight. Use me again, Lord. Make me new tomorrow morning and ready to serve You wholeheartedly. Amen.

Strength in the Lord

I can do all this through him
who gives me strength.
PHILIPPIANS 4:13 NIV

———————●———————

Lord, You are the God who gives me strength. Certainly, it is good to strengthen my body. I know I need to make time for exercise. Eating healthy is the big trend today, and it is not a bad one. I seek to improve my physical health. It makes me more productive, and it honors You. But Lord, You strengthen my soul within me. Your Word is my daily bread. When I spend time with You, I find that the day is better. My daily workout is to dig deep into scripture and meditate upon Your words. It is as simple as that. Strengthen me, Lord, even as I sleep tonight, and bring me a new day to walk boldly in my faith regardless of the circumstances. Some days are harder than others, but You are always at my side, giving me courage. I thank You for that, Father. I can do all things in Your strength. Amen.

Relying on God

*"Therefore I tell you, do not worry about your
life, what you will eat or drink; or about your
body, what you will wear. Is not life more than
food, and the body more than clothes? Look at
the birds of the air; they do not sow or reap or
store away in barns, and yet your heavenly
Father feeds them. Are you not much more
valuable than they? Can any one of you by
worrying add a single hour to your life?"*

MATTHEW 6:25–27 NIV

———

Lord, You are fully capable of taking care of me,
and yet I spend a lot of time worrying about
my daily needs. I fear financial issues and ago-
nize over what to wear to this or that event. I
feel guilty if I do not stick to a diet. I spend so
much time organizing calendars and menus that
I often miss life, don't I? Bring balance to my
planning, Father. Remove my desire to control.
Show me the way to live dependent upon You
to meet my needs, just as the birds of the air
do. Thank You for this day and give me peaceful
rest, I pray, free of worry and overplanning. In
Jesus' name, amen.

Courageous Faith

For the Spirit God gave us does not make us timid,
but gives us power, love and self-discipline.

2 TIMOTHY 1:7 NIV

———◆———

Lord, You offer a spirit of power, love, and self-discipline to me. I reach out now with a timid hand, almost afraid to hope it can be true. I lay down fear. I relinquish worry. I cast aside despair. Like the trapeze artist high above the crowd, I swing out on faith. I leave the familiar landing where I shake, afraid of falling, and I fly! My hands take hold of Your promises. I am filled with God power, God love, God discipline! I am made new. On my own, I am a schoolgirl hiding in the restroom until lunch period ends and I can blend in again. But with You, I stand up. I stand out. I shout. I share the good news. You have not made me to hide. You have made me for great adventure as You help me navigate this life. When I wake up tomorrow, remind me not to look back. I trade timidity for courage. In Jesus' name, amen.

A Hope and a Future

"For I know the plans I have for you," declares the
LORD, *"plans to prosper you and not to harm you,
plans to give you hope and a future."*

JEREMIAH 29:11 NIV

Lord, You have plans for me. Only a loving Father would have plans. Like the daddy who volunteers to coach the team and takes his daughter by the hand, heading for the soccer field, we head out, You and I, into my future. You don't sit on the sidelines. You get in the game with me. You cheer when I am victorious. The goals are more fun to score because You are there, shouting out my name. When the competition is beating me up, You turn it around for good. When I lose, You remind me there is always tomorrow. God, You are such a gracious Lord to make good plans for me. Give me rest tonight and lead me, day by day, hope filled, into the future You have for me. Amen.

Holding Hands with God

"For I am the Lord your God who takes
hold of your right hand and says to you,
Do not fear; I will help you."

ISAIAH 41:13 NIV

God, You tell me You will take hold of my hand.
You tell me not to fear and that You will help
me. There is so much packed into this one verse
of scripture. You are my Abba Father, my Daddy.
I claim these promises for my night and for tomorrow. I will not fear the darkness. I will rest in
my Abba Father's care. I will not fear tomorrow
because I know You walk with me. Not only do
You walk beside me, You reach out and take my
hand in Yours. To do life hand in hand with the
Maker of the universe is a pretty powerful thing,
I'd say. You speak to me. You tell me not to fear.
I listen. I walk. I feel Your strong hand in mine,
and I choose rest over worry. You are with me,
and that makes life a completely different experience. In Jesus' name, amen.

Pass through the Waters

"When you pass through the waters, I will be with you; and when you pass through the rivers, they will not sweep over you. When you walk through the fire, you will not be burned; the flames will not set you ablaze."

ISAIAH 43:2 NIV

Lord, sometimes the night overwhelms me. I make it through the day because I am busy, but I fear going to sleep. I don't want to toss and turn yet again. The hours pass so slowly. I feel like I am drowning. I find comfort in Your Word when You assure me that You are with me when I pass through the waters. Passing through sounds pretty good right now. Passing through says I am not going under. I will come out of this and see a new day. The waters will not sweep over me. The night will not consume me. Thank You, Father, for being with me—always. Bring me rest now, I pray, as I learn to trust You. In Jesus' name I pray, amen.

Trusting God's Timing

*There is a time for everything, and a season
for every activity under the heavens.*

ECCLESIASTES 3:1 NIV

———◆———

God, help me to rest in Your timing. I sometimes try to run ahead, and other times I hold
back and fall behind. Teach me instead to walk
in step with You, day by day. You tell me there
is a time for everything. I know Your timing is
always perfect. I know that in theory, but I find
it hard to live it out in the day to day. Help me
to trust that when Your answer to my prayer is
to wait, that You have Your reasons—and they
are for my good. Allow me to rest this night
in the knowledge that You are in control. My
worry and angst will not help the situation at
all! Help me to find solace in Your sovereignty.
Help me to allow You to work in my life in
Your timing, and help me to accept Your will.
I want what You want for my life, Lord, even
though at times I find it hard not to question
You. I do trust You, and I long to trust You more.
In Jesus' name, amen.

The Lord Will Fight for Me

"The LORD will fight for you;
you need only to be still."

EXODUS 14:14 NIV

Lord, what a promise You have shown me in this verse of scripture. You will fight for me? I need only to be still? Wow, how completely opposite this is to what the world teaches me! The world says put on your punching gloves. The world says fight for the best, climb the ladder, keep up with the Joneses. You say to rest. You say to stay still. You say to embrace peace. You say you will enter the ring on my behalf. You say leave the fighting to You! Father, as I lay me down to sleep tonight, I pray my soul You will keep. I pray You will bring a calm and a rest over my soul. I pray You will allow me to wake up tomorrow and go into my day at peace. You fight for me. I need only to be still. In Jesus' name I thank You for this promise, amen.

The Lord Is with Me

"The LORD himself goes before you and will be with you; he will never leave you nor forsake you. Do not be afraid; do not be discouraged."

DEUTERONOMY 31:8 NIV

Lord, as I go to sleep tonight, I find peace in the knowledge that You go before me into tomorrow. I am not there yet, but You are. You are the Alpha and the Omega, the beginning and the end. You see my past, present, and future. To You none of them are a mystery. Knowing You are with me as I rest and you are with me when I rise makes life sweet and peaceful for me. I trust in You, Father. Thank You for the promise that You will never leave me alone. You will never turn Your back on me. You will keep on keeping on. You will go ahead of me not just into tomorrow but into the next day and the next and the next. You are a good God, and I am blessed to be Your daughter. I will lay down discouragement and take up hope. I will trade fear for confidence. In Jesus' name, amen.

Christ Makes the Difference

*For God so loved the world that he gave his
one and only Son, that whoever believes in
him shall not perish but have eternal life.*

JOHN 3:16 NIV

———————

God, You loved us so much You sent Your only
Son. That is not a worldly love. That is a love
that only comes from You. Each day I walk in
the power of Christ Jesus. As I go to bed tonight,
I dwell upon the blessing of being set apart as
a Christ follower. The world does not know the
peace Christians know. I cannot imagine if my
only hope lay in the world. This world is not where
I place my trust because the world will always
let me down. I thank You that I was drawn to
Christ, led to salvation, chosen to receive eternal life. What grace You have poured out freely
upon my life. Thank You for loving me so. Thank
You that I never have to fear death. I will not
perish but have eternal life with You in heaven.
I cling to this promise tonight. I trust in You
as I lay my head on my pillow. Give me rest, I
pray. Amen.

Free in Christ

*"So if the Son sets you free,
you will be free indeed."*

JOHN 8:36 NIV

———— ⋅•⋅ ————

Jesus, I am free in You. Freedom feels really good.
I see so many people around me who are bound.
They are bound to work and addictions and unhealthy relationships. They are bound to worry
and fear, scurrying here and there trying the
next program and plan. They are even bound to
religion, following rules they believe You impose
upon their lives when You offer them grace in
a package so glorious it is impossible to miss—
but they do. Thank You for showing mercy to
me. Thank You for finding me in chains and
setting me free from sin. Thank You for true
freedom that is only found in You. Help me to
rest now in freedom and to walk in it as the sun
rises again tomorrow morning. I love You, Lord,
and I love the freedom You bring to my life.
Amen.

Redeemed

Then they cried to the Lord in their trouble, and he saved them from their distress. He brought them out of darkness, the utter darkness, and broke away their chains. Let them give thanks to the Lord for his unfailing love and his wonderful deeds for mankind, for he breaks down gates of bronze and cuts through bars of iron.

PSALM 107:13–16 NIV

Lord, You declare that the redeemed should stand up and tell their stories. Let the redeemed of the Lord say so! I will tell the story of my salvation all the days of my life. Just as You freed the Israelites from slavery in Egypt, You have freed my soul from sin. Each salvation has a story, and each of the plots climax with a Savior who didn't stay on the cross but rose from the dead three days after they crucified Him! You brought us out of darkness. You broke down gates of bronze. You cut through bars of iron. You would go to any length to redeem Your own. I praise You for the redemption of my soul. I rest in You now as I go to sleep. You are my peace and my rest, Lord. Amen.

Ask, Seek, Knock

"For everyone who asks receives; the one who seeks finds; and to the one who knocks, the door will be opened."

LUKE 11:10 NIV

Father, I asked and received. I sought and found. I knocked, and the door was opened to me. I am found in You. I am at rest. I can live day to day knowing that You are in control and that I will be okay. I trust in You as my Savior. You have saved me not just from eternal damnation and fire, but You have saved me from an earthly life spent scrambling on my own. I am never alone. I walk with the King of kings. I seek You in the morning and as I close each day. I climb into bed and say my prayers. I rest assured that regardless of what the night may bring, You are here. And whatever tomorrow may hold, we will face it together. Thank You for that assurance, Father. In Jesus' name, amen.

Promises of Christ

I pray that out of his glorious riches he may
strengthen you with power through his Spirit
in your inner being, so that Christ may dwell in
your hearts through faith. And I pray that you,
being rooted and established in love, may have
power, together with all the Lord's holy people,
to grasp how wide and long and high and deep
is the love of Christ, and to know this love that
surpasses knowledge—that you may be filled
to the measure of all the fullness of God.

EPHESIANS 3:16–19 NIV

Christ Jesus, You dwell in my heart through faith.
I am rooted and established in love. I have the
power to grasp the depth of Your love. I have that
power along with all of God's people. Together,
we experience the fullness of God. We live out
this life not in timidity, but in power. Not in
fear, but in faith. Bless me tonight, I ask, with a
deep and worry-free sleep. Remind me of Your
abiding love for me that says, *"Come to me, you*
who are weary. Find rest." And so tonight I take
You up on that promise. I love You, Lord. Amen.

Promise Keeper

*Not one of all the LORD's good promises
to Israel failed; every one was fulfilled.*

JOSHUA 21:45 NIV

———— ••• ————

Lord, not one of Your promises to Israel failed.
Not one. Every one was fulfilled. You are a promise keeper. And so tonight, as my heart is troubled,
I trade my hurts for Your healing and my fear
for faith. I remember Your promise that You
will never let me go. I dwell on the truth that
You know me fully and that You have plans to
prosper me and never to bring me harm. I focus
on Your promise that You will come again and
make all things right. There will be no more tears
one day. You have said it, and it is true. I find
comfort in Your promise to strengthen me, and
in that strength I can soar again, as if on eagles'
wings. I claim Your promises as I drift off to
sleep tonight and my soul finds rest within me.
Amen.

Wisdom from God

Do not let wisdom and understanding out
of your sight, preserve sound judgment and
discretion; they will be life for you, an ornament
to grace your neck. Then you will go on your
way in safety, and your foot will not stumble.
When you lie down, you will not be afraid;
when you lie down, your sleep will be sweet.

PROVERBS 3:21–24 NIV

———◆———

God, grant me wisdom. Give me sound judgment and make me discerning. Grant me discretion. May I find life and safety in these gifts that can come only from You. May I sleep sweetly tonight because I am a child of the God who shows me the way to live. Through reading Your Word and seeking You day in and day out, I find peace and guidance that are so necessary for life in this world. May I never forsake the wisdom You give to me. May it guide me always. I love You, Lord. Thank You that I find my rest in You. Amen.

Secure in Christ

He lifted me out of the slimy pit, out of
the mud and mire; he set my feet on a
rock and gave me a firm place to stand.
PSALM 40:2 NIV

God, I remember the pit. I remember the muck
and mire. I can still feel the darkness of sin and the
depths of despair, but now they are but memories.
I stand secure on the rock of Jesus Christ. My
feet are planted on a firm foundation, and I am
secure in my salvation. Thank You for saving me
and for assuring me that my salvation is solid and
permanent. I rest assured in that tonight, and I
lift up to you all of my loved ones that are still
lost. Work in their lives, I pray. I ask You to do
whatever must be done to bring them to their
knees. Humble them, Lord. Draw them to You.
I long for them to know the joy and peace and
true rest that I have found. I rest in Jesus now
and close my eyes to sleep. Amen.

Knowing God by Name

Those who know your name trust in you, for you,
LORD, have never forsaken those who seek you.

PSALM 9:10 NIV

———•———

God, there is something special about being called by name. It makes me feel known. It makes me feel singled out and important. Do You like to be called by name also? I am thankful to know Your name. To know You means to never be alone. It means to have a best friend at my side every day. It means abundant life here on this earth and eternal life in heaven. To know You means that when I am in trouble, I can call out to You. It means someone to trust in and count on. It means I never sit alone, walk alone, or fight alone. You are with me through the day, and You watch over me through the night. Give me rest tonight, I pray. Thank You for knowing me intimately and by my name, and thank You for allowing me to know You as well. Amen.

The Lord Is Peace

*Then Gideon built an altar there to the LORD
and named it The LORD is Peace. To this day
it is still in Ophrah of the Abiezrites.*

JUDGES 6:24 NASB

———◆———

Jehovah-shalom, You are my peace. I call upon
You tonight, using this, one of Your most divine
names. I ask You for a deep, abiding peace that
can only be known by a Christian. . .because
it can only come from you. Help me to rest in
that peace as I go to sleep tonight. The day
brought strain and stress, as is so often the case,
but the nighttime calls me to rest. My body is
weary and I need to sleep, but I find it hard to
control the spinning wheels of my overloaded
mind. Bring rest to me, Father. Fill me with peace
and renew my spirit within me that tomorrow
might find me ready to take on another day
with You at my side. In the Savior's name I ask,
amen.

My Healer

And He said, "If you will give earnest heed to the voice of the LORD your God, and do what is right in His sight, and give ear to His commandments, and keep all His statutes, I will put none of the diseases on you which I have put on the Egyptians; for I, the LORD, am your healer."

EXODUS 15:26 NASB

———

Jehovah-rapha, the God who heals, I call on You tonight. I need healing. I need the deep spiritual healing that can only come from You. Meet me here in my weakness. Find me, God, in this dark place. I have lost sight of You. I have neglected prayer and the reading of Your Word. I find myself depressed and in need of my Healer who promises to be the lifter of my head. Restore to me the joy of my salvation, I ask. Set me on a healthy path again. I long to worship You as I used to. I long to cast this anxiety and worry at Your feet, but I can't do it in my own strength. I need Your help. Thank You for healing me in the past. Please do so again, I ask. Amen.

The Great I Am

Then Moses said to God, "Behold, I am going to the sons of Israel, and I will say to them, 'The God of your fathers has sent me to you.' Now they may say to me, 'What is His name?' What shall I say to them?" God said to Moses, "I AM WHO I AM"; and He said, "Thus you shall say to the sons of Israel, 'I AM has sent me to you.'"

EXODUS 3:13–14 NASB

———————

Great I Am, You were with Moses. You met his needs in the wilderness. You enabled him to lead. So many years later, You are still "I Am." You tell me that You are what I need in each and every moment of the day. You whisper to me when I feel alone. You tell me: *"I am enough. I am with you."* You fill in the gaps of my life. You bind up my wounds. You fulfill me. You are merciful, Father, and when I am in need, You come to me. You are my King of glory, and You are my Prince of peace. You are like no other, and I will worship You all of my days. Tonight my need is sleep, and I trust You to provide it. Thank You for the nighttime when our bodies and minds can rest. Amen.

Abba, Father

*And because we are his children, God has
sent the Spirit of his Son into our hearts,
prompting us to call out, "Abba, Father."*

GALATIANS 4:6 NLT

Abba Father, You are God and You are also Daddy. You are a Daddy God. Holy and sovereign and to be revered and respected, yet so close. . .so willing to be known. . .so eager to help. . .so loving. . . . I think of the best daddies I have known in this life. They hold their children. They smother them with love and yet discipline them appropriately. They don't sit back watching their kids but roll up their sleeves and work with them, play with them, live life with them. This is who You are to me. You are ever present. You are always there. You cheer me on and show me the way. You walk with me. You take time for me. I am so blessed to serve a God who is also my Daddy. I love You, Abba Father. Goodnight, Lord. Thank You for watching over me as I go to sleep. Amen.

The God Who Sees Me

Thereafter, Hagar used another name to refer to the LORD, who had spoken to her. She said, "You are the God who sees me." She also said, "Have I truly seen the One who sees me?"

GENESIS 16:13 NLT

El Roi, You are the God who sees me. You see me when I am on top of the world, and You see me when it crashes in around me. You chase after me. You come close. You are kind and caring and compassionate. Just as Hagar ran away, feeling hurt and betrayed, I try to run away at times. I find myself trying to be an island, but that is not the life You intend for me. You don't leave me alone. You follow me. You surround me with grace and care. You never abandon me to fend for myself, even when I am the one who got myself into the mess. You see me even when I feel invisible. And You care. Thank You for that, God. See me now. Meet me here and bless me with rest for my weary bones. I love You, Lord. Thank You for being the God who sees me. It feels good to be seen. Amen.

El Shaddai, God Almighty

Those who live in the shelter of the Most High will find rest in the shadow of the Almighty. This I declare about the Lord: He alone is my refuge, my place of safety; he is my God, and I trust him.

PSALM 91:1–2 NLT

El Shaddai, God Almighty, You are all-powerful. You are mighty, and I find rest in Your shadow. Like a child walking hand in hand with her daddy, I look up and notice that Your shadow is so much larger than my own. You are a great God. You are El Shaddai. You make me feel safe. You can be trusted. I am assured of security because I am Your child. You go before me, walk with me, and cover me from behind. Day after day You provide for me a shelter and rest that only You can provide. Keep me close tonight. Hold me, almighty God. Remind me that because I dwell in Your shadow, I am safe and secure. Amen.

The Lord Is My Banner

*Moses built an altar there and named
it Yahweh-Nissi (which means
"the LORD is my banner").*

EXODUS 17:15 NLT

Yahweh Nissi, You are my Protector. You lead, and You deliver me from those who come against me. You are my Banner. Just as You provided supernatural victory for Your people when they fought the Amalekites, You will provide the same for me. I raise my hands to You. I will give You all the glory when I defeat sins that seek to ensnare me. I call upon You, my Banner. Save me from the desire to lose myself in social media. Free me from the belief that the number of likes on my posts determines my worth. Give me victory over whatever addiction may nip at my heels. Go before me into battle as I fight to remain pure. Yahweh Nissi, I call You by name. I recognize Your power. I rest in it tonight. Fight for me. I know that I need only to be still. Amen.

Day and Night

*The wise counsel God gives when I'm awake
is confirmed by my sleeping heart. Day and
night I'll stick with God; I've got a good
thing going and I'm not letting go.*

PSALM 16:7–8 MSG

I trust You in the daytime, God, and I trust You
through the night. You counsel me throughout
the day. I find moments to turn to You in prayer,
and I sense Your presence there with me, help-
ing me to know what to do. In the night, You
do not leave my side. You watch over me. You
protect and guide my thoughts even as I sleep.
I wake up, refreshed and ready for a new day. I
don't want to find out what life would be like
without my God leading me day and night. Just
like the Israelites were led through a cloud in
the daytime and by a pillar of fire at night, I am
led by Your Holy Spirit and walk in the paths
of righteousness. I love You, Lord, thank You
for always being with me. Amen.

Hope

*We who have taken refuge would have
strong encouragement to take hold of the
hope set before us. This hope we have as
an anchor of the soul, a hope both sure and
steadfast and one which enters within the veil.*

HEBREWS 6:18–19 NASB

———— • ————

Your Word encourages me to take hold of the
hope. Tonight I picture hope like an anchor
thrown out to hold a fishing boat in place so
that it doesn't drift away. It is secure. I know that
hope is something to be treasured. And tonight
though I feel lost on the surface, deep below in
the recesses of my heart I can feel the security.
And I recall that I have a steadfast anchor in
Jesus. You are here with me, Lord, through the
storms. When there is nothing else for me, there
You are, my anchor. I close my eyes and know
that You are here with me. When there is little
hope that I can see, I know You are with me as
my anchor, my Deliverer, my hope. Amen.

Fearfully and Wonderfully Made

For You formed my inward parts; You wove me in my mother's womb. I will give thanks to You, for I am fearfully and wonderfully made; wonderful are Your works, and my soul knows it very well.

PSALM 139:13–14 NASB

God, You made me. Your Word says that You knit me together in my mother's womb. I know that I am fearfully and wonderfully made. If You made me, certainly You know me better than anyone else knows me. I thank You for creating me just the way I am and blessing me with the gifts and abilities You chose just for me. Even though on occasion I wish something was different about my physical appearance or I feel envious of someone else's gifting, deep down I like being me! Please encourage my spirit tonight and remind me that You love me exactly as I am. As I go to bed, I praise Your holy name and give You thanks. Amen.

A Way Out

*No temptation has overtaken you but such as is
common to man; and God is faithful, who will not
allow you to be tempted beyond what you are able,
but with the temptation will provide the way of
escape also, so that you will be able to endure it.*

1 CORINTHIANS 10:13 NASB

———————————

Faithful God, I come to You tonight praising Your name and thanking You for being so loyal to Your children. You always provide a way out when I am tempted. I always have the opportunity to say no and to avoid sin in my life. Christian men and women for generations have endured some of the same temptations I face today. What a blessing to know that You will always provide an escape route for me when I am tempted. Before I go to sleep tonight, I confess that there were times today I chose to sin. The words were out of my mouth or the action taken before I could stop myself. Give me strength tomorrow to say no to sin. You are my way out! In Jesus' name I pray, amen.

Every Good and Perfect Gift

*Every good thing given and every perfect
gift is from above, coming down from
the Father of lights, with whom there
is no variation or shifting shadow.*

JAMES 1:17 NASB

God, You are a great gift giver. I think about my
friend who is such an expert gift selector. She
does such a great job of choosing a pair of ear-
rings or a scarf for each friend because she knows
their preferences. She has become a student of
people. She cares about the details. Mary looks
good in blue. Susan prefers gold to silver jewelry.
That's how You are, God. You know each of
Your children so well. You put each of us together.
You know our favorites and our desires. And You
know how to give us good gifts. Sometimes You
even give us gifts we did not know we needed—
like that surprise third child or the job promo-
tion we would never have expected! Every
good and perfect gift comes from Your hands.
Tonight I thank You for the gifts in my life. I
thank You especially for my salvation through
Jesus and my abundant life through Him. Amen.

God Is Truth

"God is not a man, that He should lie,
nor a son of man, that He should repent.
Has He said, and will He not do? Or has
He spoken, and will He not make it good?"

NUMBERS 23:19 NKJV

———————

Heavenly Father, You set the standard for truth.
You are not a man. You always keep Your word.
Man is not capable of such utter honesty and
devotion and yet, we are made in Your image.
Made in Your image, we bear some of Your
traits. We can choose to strive to live a life known
for strong character and honesty. Help me, I
pray, to look a little more like You each day.
Tomorrow morning when I wake up, I will have
opportunities to be honest all day long. Even
in small ways, Father, such as returning the
change when the cashier gives me too much. I
want to live a life of truth. You are my standard.
You are Truth. In Jesus' name, amen.

God's Word

"This Book of the Law shall not depart from your mouth, but you shall meditate in it day and night, that you may observe to do according to all that is written in it. For then you will make your way prosperous, and then you will have good success."

JOSHUA 1:8 NKJV

———— ● ————

Lord, You tell me to meditate on Your Word day and night. I must know it and know it well in order to observe the commands that are written in it. I must read it regularly in order to live according to Your will. Father, I am guilty of taking the Bible for granted, and yet I know in some places people do not have easy access to scripture. Teach me to respect Your Word and to desire to read it daily. Tonight I begin by reading just one chapter. I know that as I read Your Word, there will be great reward in my life. I am promised that when I value Your Word in my life, you will make me prosperous and successful. What a promise! Amen.

Faithfulness

"Hear, O Israel: The LORD our God,
the LORD is one! You shall love the Lord
your God with all your heart, with all
your soul, and with all your strength."

DEUTERONOMY 6:4–5 NKJV

Lord, my God, help me to love You with all of my heart. I don't want to hold anything back. You are so faithful to Your people. You remain the same, steadfast and true. You do not shift with the wind or change with the seasons of the year. As I read Your Word, I get to know Your heart. I see Your deep love for Your children. I read the stories of heroes of the faith. They were regular people, just like me, but they each stand out with one trait. They followed hard after You. They knew Your Word. They spent time with You. Make me a woman of great faith, I ask. Give me the desire and the discipline to start right now, spending some time in Your Word and in prayer before I close this day and go to sleep. In Jesus' name, amen.

God Reveals Himself

As he journeyed he came near Damascus, and
suddenly a light shone around him from heaven.

ACTS 9:3 NKJV

God, You reveal Yourself. You showed Yourself
to Saul on the road to Damascus. Your glory
passed by as Moses hid in the cleft of the rock.
You have revealed Yourself to me as well. I have
not heard an audible voice, but there are times
when You are so close, I feel I could reach out
and touch You. Thank You for those times. I
pray tonight that I will have a special sense of
Your presence. I need to know You are near
and here with me. I love You, Lord. As I go to
sleep tonight, remind me of Your faithfulness
through the years. I will follow You all the days
of my life. Amen.

A Humble King

Who, being in very nature God, did not consider equality with God something to be used to his own advantage; rather, he made himself nothing by taking the very nature of a servant, being made in human likeness. And being found in appearance as a man, he humbled himself by becoming obedient to death—even death on a cross!

PHILIPPIANS 2:6–8 NIV

Jesus, You came as a baby, born in a lowly stable. You left heaven to come down here with us. You were the King of kings, but You chose a quiet entrance into this world. You did not come with grandeur but with simplicity. You are a Savior we can draw near to and talk to and confide in. You walked on this earth as a man. You "get" humanity. Thank You for that, Savior. Thank You for humbling Yourself as no other king has ever or will ever do. You endured persecution, beating, and even a horrible death out of Your great love for me. I take great comfort as I go to sleep tonight, knowing that You would go to such extremes to make me Your own. I love You, Jesus. Amen.

Help Me to Forgive

Then Peter came and said to Him, "Lord, how often shall my brother sin against me and I forgive him? Up to seven times?" Jesus said to him, "I do not say to you, up to seven times, but up to seventy times seven."

MATTHEW 18:21–22 NASB

Lord, I come to You tonight hurt. I find it so hard to forgive those who mistreat me. But in these quiet moments as I meditate upon Your Word, I dwell upon Your grace and see You before me on that cross, carrying my sin willingly upon Your sinless self. I know that You tell me to forgive again and again, seventy times seven. Give me the grace to do so, Lord Jesus. Help me to imitate You in my ability to forgive. I want to live free of the resentment that has built up inside of my heart. I know from experience that when I finally do forgive, there is a huge weight lifted. Free me of bitterness, I ask. In Your precious name I pray, amen.

Root Out Bitterness

Bearing with one another, and forgiving each
other, whoever has a complaint against anyone;
just as the Lord forgave you, so also should you.
COLOSSIANS 3:13 NASB

———◆———

Lord, I toss and turn in my bed at night. I remember the hurt and the pain of the wrongdoing, and I just cannot rest. I want to release it. I truly do. I wish that I could be more forgiving on my own, but I have tried and I keep coming up short. I need Your help. I need You to soften my heart and change me from the inside out. I know that You can do this because You have transformed my heart in other ways through the years. This unforgiveness is like a fever or a virus that spreads. I do not want it to infect me any further. Root out the bitterness, I pray. Help me to forgive so that my soul may find rest. In Jesus' name I pray, amen.

Confessing Sin

*If we claim that we're free of sin, we're only
fooling ourselves. A claim like that is errant
nonsense. On the other hand, if we admit our
sins—make a clean breast of them—he won't
let us down; he'll be true to himself. He'll forgive
our sins and purge us of all wrongdoing. If we
claim that we've never sinned, we out-and-out
contradict God—make a liar out of him. A claim
like that only shows off our ignorance of God.*

1 JOHN 1:8–10 MSG

———

God, no one is free of sin. No one except You. I
come before You tonight, confessing that I have
fallen short of Your glory yet again. It is my sin
nature. It constantly opposes my desire to do
what is right, and sometimes it wins. Forgive
me, and help me to turn from sin. I admit my
wrongdoing, and I cling to the cross of Christ
that made a way for me to come before You. I
am righteous only through His blood. On my
own, I could never reach a holy God. Forgive
me, Father, and make me clean. Amen.

Repentance

*"Now repent of your sins and turn to God,
so that your sins may be wiped away."*

ACTS 3:19 NLT

Lord, You are able to forgive my sin. You tell me in Your Word that You will wipe it away and remember it no longer if I will just confess and turn from my sin. You promise to remove my sin as far as the east is from the west. You call me to repentance. Like a teacher sweeps an eraser across the board and has a fresh, clean surface upon which to write again, You promise to blot out my transgressions. Each time I return to You and repent of sin, I find a clean slate, a fresh start, a new beginning with You. I am so thankful for that, Father. Forgive me now as I speak the sins of this day before You. I turn from sin and I ask for Your help when I wake in the morning to do better in the coming day. Amen.

Life Transformation

This means that anyone who belongs to
Christ has become a new person. The
old life is gone; a new life has begun!
2 CORINTHIANS 5:17 NLT

———————————•———————————

Lord, life transformation is an amazing thing! More miraculous than the mystery of the caterpillar turning into a beautiful butterfly is the way You soften the hearts of people. I have heard so many believers share their powerful testimonies of life transformation. Each story is different, but each one bears witness to Your ability to utterly alter an existence. You changed Saul into Paul on the road to Damascus. You reach into prison cells. You snatch souls out of deep, dark addictions. You find the sharpest-looking business professional and root out the sin that rules in his heart. Regardless of the story, they all begin with sin and end with forgiveness. Thank You for completely changing my life. As I lay my head down tonight, I thank You for my righteousness through Christ. Amen.

God Chooses to Forget

Then he says, "I will never again remember
their sins and lawless deeds." And when
sins have been forgiven, there is no
need to offer any more sacrifices.
HEBREWS 10:17–18 NLT

God, You are all-knowing and all-powerful. You
have a mind that could retain worlds of information, and yet You choose to forget. You promise
me in Your Word that You will forget and never
again remember my sin. Your Son died on the
cross, and because I believe in Him, there is no
need for any further sacrifice to be offered. He
died once, for all. He covered all my sin in that act.
How thankful I am that You forgive and forget.
Father, forgive me of the sins of this day. Cast
them as far as the east is from the west. Recall
them no more, I ask. Lead me into tomorrow
with a fresh start and make my life pleasing to
You. In the powerful name of the Messiah, Jesus,
I pray. Amen.

Praying as Jesus Taught Me to Pray

"This, then, is how you should pray: 'Our
Father in heaven, hallowed be your name,
your kingdom come, your will be done,
on earth as it is in heaven. Give us today our
daily bread. And forgive us our debts, as we also
have forgiven our debtors. And lead us not into
temptation, but deliver us from the evil one.'"

MATTHEW 6:9–13 NIV

———

Lord, in heaven, Your name is holy. I look forward to the day You come again, and until then I pray for Your will to be done on earth. Please provide for my needs through this night and take care of me tomorrow. Thank You for Your provision for me. Forgive my sin, Lord, as I forgive those who sin against me. Give me an escape route when I am weighed down by temptation to sin, Father. You promise me in Your Word that You will always give me a way out. Keep Satan away from my life, I ask in the powerful name of the Savior, Jesus Christ. Amen.

Encourage One Another

Therefore encourage one another and build each other up, just as in fact you are doing.

1 THESSALONIANS 5:11 NIV

Lord, make me an encourager. I have found so much encouragement from You and from believers that You have put on my path. So many times, when I have been at my wit's end, I have received a word from a friend or a special touch from Your hand in a unique way that helps me. I want, in turn, to build others up. As I rest before You tonight, bring to mind those in my life that I might encourage. Show me my coworkers, neighbors, and friends whose spirits need to be lifted. Bring to mind family members who need a special reminder of Your great love this week. Then show me, Father, tangible ways that I can be an encourager. I want to bless others as I have been blessed in this way. In Jesus' name I ask, amen.

Peace Giver

Praise the LORD! He has kept his promise
and given us peace. Every good thing he
promised to his servant Moses has happened.

1 KINGS 8:56 CEV

———————◆———————

Lord, I come to You tonight with a heart full
of praise. I praise You for keeping Your promises. You are a promise keeper. So unlike many
people in this world today, You keep Your cov-
enants. You stand by Your Word. Thank You
for being the giver of great peace. I bask in that
peace tonight, even though my life has its ups
and downs, because peace is the constant beneath
the surface. It is the reason I can rest easy in my
bed tonight. It is the knowledge that no matter
what comes my way in the coming days, You are
with me and I am okay. In Jesus' name I praise and
thank You tonight for giving me peace. Amen.

God Is My Power Source

He gives strength to the weary
and increases the power of the weak.
ISAIAH 40:29 NIV

Lord, I imagine myself in a fight. The enemies are piled on. Things are not in my favor. It's not looking good. And then, suddenly, You swoop in. Like a superhero extraordinaire, You zap me with extra strength. You increase my power. And bam! I stand up. My adversaries run back in amazement. Their eyes are wide. I once was so very weak, and they had the upper hand. Suddenly, I am courageous and confident. My God showed up. He gave me strength when I was weary. He increased my power when I was weak. Lord, You are the power source. When I am tapped into that source by staying close to You, reading Your Word, and spending time in prayer, I always come out on top. Nothing can keep me down. I thank You for that as I close this day. May You give me strength even as I sleep, and when I wake tomorrow morning, please give me endurance for another day, no matter what it brings. Amen.

Covenant of Love

*Know therefore that the LORD your God is
God; he is the faithful God, keeping his covenant
of love to a thousand generations of those who
love him and keep his commandments.*

DEUTERONOMY 7:9 NIV

God, this covenant of love is nothing new to
You. You have kept Your promises for generations. Your eyes watch over the land for those
who love You and keep Your commandments.
You walk close with us. You bless us. You love
us with an unfathomable, unconditional love.
As I lie down tonight to rest my weary soul, I
take comfort in the fact that You have been at
this a long time! You were faithful to Abraham
and Isaac. You were faithful to Moses. You kept
Your covenant of love to the New Testamen
disciples. There are footprints of faith down
through the ages, those who have followed hard
after You, and beside them in the sand are the
tracings of sovereign sandals, the prints of our
unchanging God. Thank You for Your great
love. It sustains me day by day. In Jesus' name,
amen.

Hold Unswervingly to Hope

Let us hold unswervingly to the hope we
profess, for he who promised is faithful.

HEBREWS 10:23 NIV

Heavenly Father, I remember learning to ride a bike. I would swerve to the left and then to the right. There was nothing steady or sure about my ride! But then that faithful adult in my life grabbed hold of the back of the bicycle. Suddenly, I was on the sidewalk, cruising straight down the center, feeling like I could ride forever! What a difference it made to have someone directing me, someone holding on tight, someone providing structure and steadiness to my adventure. You are my hope. You hold on to the back of my bike. I am sure and steady when I have You there, and the best part is You never let go. Faithful God, You never turn me loose to do it on my own. I will hold unswervingly to the hope that I profess. Give me rest tonight. Peaceful rest that comes to those who trust in You. Amen.

God Is Perfectly Faithful

Lord, you are my God; I will exalt you and praise
your name, for in perfect faithfulness you have
done wonderful things, things planned long ago.

ISAIAH 25:1 NIV

———————

Lord, my God, I come before You tonight exalting
You and praising Your name. You are perfectly
faithful. Not much in this world is perfect. There's
a whole lot of imperfect, in fact! I lead an imperfect life in the midst of an imperfect family.
I do an imperfect job at an imperfect workplace.
There are flaws in my relationships, and my days
include the errors of sin. All of them. Even on
my best day, I am a sinner. But You, Lord, do
wonderful things. You keep blessing me in spite
of my spiritual temperature. You are perfectly
faithful. You are perfectly true. And so tonight
I rest easy, knowing that while I am imperfect,
I am perfectly loved by a perfectly loyal Lord
who will never change with the shifting shadows
of the night. In Jesus' name I pray, amen.

Increase My Faith

And He said to them, "Why are you
afraid? Do you still have no faith?"

MARK 4:40 NASB

———◆———

Lord, the disciples had seen You perform miracles.
You had fed thousands from a handful of fish and
bread, enabled the lame to walk and the blind to
see. But they did not trust You to calm a storm
on the sea that night. I shake my head in disgust
at their lack of faith. . .until I look in the mirror.
How many miracles have I witnessed? How many
times have You undeniably intervened in my
own life and rescued me? How many times have
You healed my heart? And yet, this morning
I woke up and took the wheel, didn't I? I long for
that control. I don't trust You as I should. Like
the disciples, I panic. Are You sleeping? Have
You missed this? I am in trouble here! How
silly of me! Why am I afraid? Do I still have no
faith? Increase my faith, I pray. I don't need to
move any mountains, Lord, but I need to rest tonight. Grow my faith, I ask, and set me on course
when I wake again for a faith-filled day. Amen.

I Will Not Be Afraid

So that we confidently say, "The Lord is my helper,
I will not be afraid. What will man do to me?"
HEBREWS 13:6 NASB

———•———

Lord, I love to watch young children playing
at the park. They are so carefree and content.
They long for nothing more than to swing a bit
higher or experience the thrill of the slide once
more. Make me content like a child, Lord.
Cause me to rest assured tonight that nothing
can touch my life without coming through You
first. You are a sovereign filter. You aren't like
man who is here today and gone tomorrow. You
are the same yesterday, today, and tomorrow. You
promise never to leave or forsake me. You are
my Helper, and I need not be afraid. I do not
need to fear the darkness of night. When I wake
in the wee hours, Lord, assure me in my spirit
that You are there and that I have nothing to
fear. You've got this. You've got me in the palm
of Your hand. Amen.

The Peace of God

"Peace I leave with you, My peace I give to you;
not as the world gives do I give to you. Let not
your heart be troubled, neither let it be afraid."

JOHN 14:27 NKJV

Lord, I have sought peace in the world. I have
tried to find it in relationships, but they end,
or at best disappoint. Even the lasting ones are
flawed. They are not enough. Other people cannot
provide peace, no matter how wonderful they
are. I have tried to find peace in my work. I make
a difference there. But at the end of the day,
when the sun goes down, the building is locked
up and it is cold stone. It does not bring me
comfort. It would not miss me if I did not show
up the next morning. You are the peace giver. You
give peace that this world does not have to offer.
Like name-brand jeans purchased just from one
source, your peace is unique. It stands out. It is
nothing like the generic version. I know from
experience. I have tried both on for size, and there
is no comparison. Fill me with that everlasting
peace tonight. I need a strong dose of it. I love
You, Lord. Thank You for giving me peace. Amen.

Direct My Paths

In all your ways acknowledge Him,
and He shall direct your paths.

PROVERBS 3:6 NKJV

———•———

Father, tonight I come to You. I acknowledge You as Lord of all. I call out Your name. I need to sense Your presence ever near. I believe You are God and You are real. I believe You are in heaven and right here with me now. You are omnipotent, omniscient, all-powerful, all-knowing. I need the rest and peace that only You can give. I am unsure which way to go. There are endless choices. I tend toward the comfortable path more than the one that requires risk. But I so greatly fear missing what You may have for me on the road less traveled. Direct my paths, God. Set me on the best course. I want to honor You with my life and with each choice I make. As I call on You tonight, I ask You to give me guidance. Give me comfort and rest. Assure me, yet again, that You are in control and that You will never leave me. In Jesus' name I thank You for Your direction. Amen.

God Came to Me

"I will not leave you orphans;
I will come to you."
JOHN 14:18 NKJV

Lord, You came to me. You did not leave me comfortless. You showed up. You rolled up Your sleeves. You came alongside me. You know the itch of manger hay. It was Your bed. You did that for me. You know the calluses of a carpenter's hands. You did not have to leave heaven's glory for callused hands, but You did. You did it for me. You know the ache of dusty, sandaled feet that have walked too many miles in one day. You are the King of kings. You could have demanded that others wash Your feet; instead, You bent and insisted on washing theirs. You came as a humble servant leader. And the best news ever is. . .that You came. You did not leave me an orphan. You are the Father of the fatherless. You adopted me into Your family. I am a daughter of the King. I bear Your image and Your name. I strive to look a little more like You, Abba Father, with each passing day. Touch my brow tonight. Whisper in my ear. Sing over me. Remind me of my identity. Give me rest, I pray. Amen.

The Lord Answers When I Call

*"Then you shall call, and the LORD will answer;
you shall cry, and He will say, 'Here I am.'"*
ISAIAH 58:9 NKJV

Lord, You answer when I call. Tonight I call out to You. I feel lost and alone. I feel empty and afraid. I need a special touch from You to make it tonight. I need the assurance that you are not just near, but here. You are not just aware, but active. I believe You are at work in my circumstances, but today I just feel so defeated. And so I cry out to my all-knowing, everlasting God. I stick my neck out. I jump in with both feet. I cling to faith because it is the only hope I have. I speak Your name. I call upon the Great I Am who has been exactly what I needed so many times in the past. You have been my King of glory on the mountaintop. Now I find myself in the valley, and I beg You to be my Prince of peace. Grant me peaceful sleep as I release my concerns to You. I love You, Lord. Thank You for answering when I call. Amen.

The Lord, My Deliverer

"Call upon Me in the day of trouble;
I will deliver you, and you shall glorify Me."

PSALM 50:15 NKJV

Great Deliverer, I call upon You in my time of trouble. I call out to You, knowing that once again You will meet me here. You are a light in the darkness. The night does not cast shadows upon Your glory. So many times before, You have rescued me. You have delivered me from temptation and from wrong choices that have led to dead ends. You have seen my distress and showed up to save the day. Better than any superhero, You soar into my scenario gone wrong and surprise me with a much better ending than I would have imagined possible. Find me here, Lord. My soul desires peaceful rest from worry. I need Your deliverance once again. I glorify You in advance because I know that my Deliverer will deliver me once again. In Jesus' name, amen.

Life Preserver

The LORD shall preserve you from all evil;
He shall preserve your soul. The LORD shall
preserve your going out and your coming in
from this time forth, and even forevermore.

PSALM 121:7–8 NKJV

Lord, You tell me in Your Word that You will preserve me from evil. You will preserve my soul. You will preserve my going out and my coming in, forever. You are my preserver. I think about a life preserver tossed to a drowning man. He thrashes and splashes, trying to save himself, but to no avail. Then, just as his energy begins to fail and he starts to go under, a life preserver comes. He clings on. He coughs. He lives. He breathes. He finds rest. His life has been preserved. Oh great life preserver, I am so thankful that in You I never have to fear the rising waters. Your angels surround me. Your watchful eye is always upon me. I will trust in You. Preserve my life, I pray. Amen.

Light and Strength

The LORD is my light and my salvation;
whom shall I fear? The LORD is the strength
of my life; of whom shall I be afraid?

PSALM 27:1 NKJV

You, Lord, are my light and my salvation. Even
in the darkness, light shines. It illuminates the
area. It brightens things up. It takes away the
shadows. It provides for clearer vision. It dispels
darkness. You, Lord, are my light giver. You are
my source of light when I find myself in the dark.
Tonight I need to see clearly. I need understanding. I need perseverance and endurance. I need
strength to go on. Because You are my light and
my Strength, I know I have nothing to fear. Why
should I fear the darkness when I am a child of
the light? Be close now, Lord. Illuminate my
situation. Guide me. Bless me. Draw me near
to You. I want to walk in confidence through
the darkness and into the light. In Jesus' name
I pray, amen.

Asking for Wisdom

If you need wisdom, ask our generous God,
and he will give it to you. He will
not rebuke you for asking.

JAMES 1:5 NLT

Generous God, You are the source of wisdom. I
come to You tonight in need of just that. I ask
You to shine Your light on my path. I need
wisdom that can come only from above. I have
learned to be still and know that You are God.
It is in the stillness that I hear Your voice. I discern Your will and Your way. I see from Your
perspective and determine right from wrong.
Illuminate my heart and mind, I ask. Give me
assurance that You are here and You care. Remove
confusion, Father, that keeps me awake at night.
I do not want to waste another night tossing and
turning. I know that You do not wish to hide
wisdom from me. You give generously to those
who ask. I am humbly asking tonight for wisdom that I simply cannot muster up or google
or search out anywhere else. You are the wisdom
source that I am tapping into. Thank You in
advance for the wisdom You will give. Amen.

Learning His Ways

Many peoples will come and say, "Come, let us go up to the mountain of the LORD, to the temple of the God of Jacob. He will teach us his ways, so that we may walk in his paths." The law will go out from Zion, the word of the LORD from Jerusalem.

ISAIAH 2:3 NIV

God of Abraham, Isaac, and Jacob. My God, my Father, my Lord, meet me here. Teach me of Your ways that I may walk in Your paths. Your ways are so different than the ways of this world. The world tells me to look out for myself, to do what feels right, to walk away if things get tough. The world whispers lies, but they sound so pretty on the lips of superstars and trained musicians. Your ways are not the ways of this world. You say that the last shall be first. You say to turn the other cheek. You bent to wash Your followers' feet. You tell me that above all, I should put on love. You tell me to forgive, seventy times seven. Lord, I seek You so that I may walk in Your ways all the days of my life. Starting with tonight. Starting with tomorrow. In Jesus' name, amen.

Instruction and Guidance from the Lord

I will instruct you and teach you in the way you should go; I will guide you with My eye.

PSALM 32:8 NKJV

Lord, You instruct me in the way I should go. I need some of that instruction tonight. I imagine the connection between a mother and child. When the mother raises an eyebrow, the child's behavior improves. When the corner of her mouth turns up, his antics increase in silliness because he has gained a smile from his greatest fan. Each story started by the mother. . .is finished by the child. He has heard her tell them all a hundred times before. They are in sync—mother and child. They have been together nearly constantly since he was born. That is a lot like Your instruction to me. You guide me with Your eye. All it takes is a nod of approval, a turn of Your head, a look in Your eye and I am quick to follow Your lead. You are my Father, and bonded through the blood of Christ, we are united. Guide me with Your eye, Father. Set me on the path. Instruct me, and I shall follow Your lead. In Jesus' name I pray, amen.

Wisdom, Knowledge, and Joy

For God gives wisdom and knowledge
and joy to a man who is good in His sight.
ECCLESIASTES 2:26 NKJV

God, I am righteous only through the blood Christ shed for me. I am good only because I am made right with You through faith, by grace. Thank You for pouring out upon me wisdom, knowledge, and joy. Gifts unmatched are these. Wisdom guides me. It is the treasured pearl, a compass, a map, a lamp. Knowledge informs me. My faith lives because of fact, truth, and enlightenment. It lifts the veil over my eyes that Your Word might spring off the page. . .I understand. Joy is the icing on the cake. It runs as deep as an ocean. Happiness is but a shallow river that may dry up tomorrow. But joy—joy is eternal, abiding, permanent, not temporal. It is unchanging. It carries me to mountaintops but endures in the valley. Wisdom, knowledge, joy. How blessed am I. I rest in these tonight and in Your grace poured out upon my soul that I might be found good in Your sight—only through Jesus. Amen.

Praying Earnestly

Now Hannah spoke in her heart; only her
lips moved, but her voice was not heard.
Therefore Eli thought she was drunk.

1 Samuel 1:13 nkjv

Lord, I come to you earnestly like my sister Hannah so many years ago. There is a void in my life. There is a longing. Hannah prayed so earnestly that she appeared drunk. She had prayed her prayer before on the temple steps. She must have believed You for great things. She kept coming. She kept asking. She kept earnestly praying. May I be found like Hannah, so involved in my prayer that I might be perceived as crazy! Meet my need, God. Fill my longing. Whether in the way I ask, or in the way You see as better, answer my prayer. I come before You tonight, fervent in prayer. Give me the endurance to keep praying, to keep believing, to keep seeking Your answer to my call. May I pray with the faith of Hannah. Even when I cannot see Your movement in my life I know that You are at work. In Jesus' name I pray, amen.

Blessing for Faithfulness

Ruth answered, "Please don't tell me to leave
you and return home! I will go where you go,
I will live where you live; your people will
be my people, your God will be my God."

RUTH 1:16 CEV

———————

Lord, I have always admired Ruth. She sacri-
ficed a lot in her loyalty to her mother-in-law.
She stuck with Naomi through thick and thin.
She would not leave her, even when it would have
been perfectly acceptable according to society.
She went into a foreign land. She went with
Naomi. She did what it took to provide for her-
self and for her aging mother-in-law. She trusted
You. And You provided. You even provided
an unexpected surprise—a husband. Boaz was
Your provision for Ruth. You saw her selflessness.
You rewarded her resolve. Your favor was upon
her for her faithfulness. Find me faithful, Lord.
Find me selfless and resolved to do what is right,
whether anyone is watching or not. I love You,
Lord. Give me a little bit of what Ruth had, I
ask tonight. In Jesus' name, amen.

Loving Those Who Are Hard to Love

We love because God loved us first.
1 JOHN 4:19 CEV

God, I come to You tonight asking You to make me more loving. I am the recipient of great love. I want to be loving as well. There are some people who are hard to love. After I have given and been hurt, after I have loved and been rejected, it is so hard to remain loving. Give me the mind of Christ. He came as a servant leader. He loved with an unfailing love that led Him all the way to the cross—even for those who persecuted Him that day. Help me to love because You first loved me. I am not justified in withholding love when it has been lavished upon me so. And so tonight, as I become still before You in these moments before bed, I bring You the names of those I want to love well. I list them out for You, although You already know. Fill my heart with love, even for those I find hardest to love. In Jesus' name I ask, amen.

Red Sea Situation

*By faith they passed through the Red
Sea as though they were passing through
dry land; and the Egyptians, when
they attempted it, were drowned.*

HEBREWS 11:29 NASB

———— ◆ ————

Lord, You show up at just the right time, never
early or late. Just as You parted the Red Sea for
the Israelites, You also allowed it to swallow up
the Egyptians who came right behind. Father,
Your power knows no bounds. I have hit a dead
end in my life, Lord. I can't imagine You could
intervene at this juncture. But I step into the past
tonight and slip on the sandals of an Israelite.
Tired from running, about to be overtaken by
angry masters and punished for my escape, I fling
myself into the shallows of the Red Sea. There
is no way out. There is no happy ending. And
then, in an instant, the waters part! I stumble
to my feet and pass through on dry land to the
other side. Glancing back, I watch my pursuers
drown. Father, meet me here at the edge of my
Red Sea. Part the waters, I pray. I rest in You
tonight, knowing that You always show up. Amen.

Find Me Ready

*"And just as it happened in the days of Noah,
so it will be also in the days of the Son of Man:
they were eating, they were drinking, they were
marrying, they were being given in marriage,
until the day that Noah entered the ark, and the
flood came and destroyed them all. It was the same
as happened in the days of Lot: they were eating,
they were drinking, they were buying, they were
selling, they were planting, they were building."*

LUKE 17:26–28 NASB

Lord, my thoughts turn to Your second coming tonight. You tell us that up until the day You return, we will be just living life. We will be going out to dinner, attending weddings of friends, and posting on social media. We will be shopping and decorating and getting our nails done. But will we be reading Your Word? Will we be found in prayer? Will we be sharing the Gospel? Father, find me ready. Give me a sense of urgency in my heart this very night. I want to be ready when You come again. Amen.

The Lord Defends Me

"The LORD is my strength and my defense; he has become my salvation. He is my God, and I will praise him, my father's God, and I will exalt him."

EXODUS 15:2 NIV

———————◆———————

God, You are my Strength and my song. You are my Salvation. I will praise You. You are my defender. Like a child on the playground being bullied, I am often weak and awkward in this world. But You come to my defense. You rescue me. You pull the bullies off of me and help me to my feet. You say that I am Yours. You tell them my name. They recognize it and step back. They cower in Your presence. You are better than any big brother coming to the rescue. You are the Lord of lords and the King of kings. And so tonight, I call upon You, my defender. I praise and exalt Your name. I lift You up. Fill me with a sense of who I am and remind me that as I go into battle tomorrow, You go before me. You are with me. You fight for me. I need only to be still. In Jesus' name I pray, amen.

Living Water

On the last and greatest day of the festival, Jesus
stood and said in a loud voice, "Let anyone who is
thirsty come to me and drink. Whoever believes in
me, as Scripture has said, rivers of living water
will flow from within them." By this he meant the
Spirit, whom those who believed in him were later
to receive. Up to that time the Spirit had not been
given, since Jesus had not yet been glorified.

JOHN 7:37–39 NIV

God, thank You for sending the Holy Spirit. The
Spirit is my Counselor and my comfort. Tonight
I am in need of that living water that Jesus spoke
of in John 7. I need the refreshment of the steady
flow, as long and wide as a river. I need the never-ending comfort of the Spirit. Please hold me
close. Renew my faith. Calm my fears. I thirst for
spiritual peace, and I know that it can be found
only in You. I know I must seek You and drink
deep of the everlasting water. Only then will I
thirst no more. You offered living water to the
woman at the well. Her life was forever changed.
Change me, Father, from the inside out. Fill me
with Your Spirit, and comfort me in these night
hours that stretch out before me, I pray. Amen.

Jesus Makes the Difference

"The One that God sent speaks God's words.
And don't think he rations out the Spirit in
bits and pieces. The Father loves the Son
extravagantly. He turned everything over
to him so he could give it away—a lavish
distribution of gifts. That is why whoever accepts
and trusts the Son gets in on everything, life
complete and forever! And that is also why the
person who avoids and distrusts the Son is in
the dark and doesn't see life. All he experiences of
God is darkness, and an angry darkness at that."

JOHN 3:34–36 MSG

God, I am so thankful. I am thankful to know You.
I am thankful You had a plan for the redemption
of man. Jesus. He is the bridge between You and
me. His blood upon the cross paid the price for
my sin. I can come, made righteous by grace
through faith, before my holy God. I lift up to
You my loved ones who continue to reject You,
Lord. How sad that they walk in utter darkness.
How I pray that they will come to know You and
be saved. Tonight, as I settle down to sleep, I bring
their names before You. Save them, Father. Amen.

Lydia

A woman named Lydia, from the city of
Thyatira, a seller of purple fabrics, a worshiper
of God, was listening; and the Lord opened her
heart to respond to the things spoken by Paul.
And when she and her household had been
baptized, she urged us, saying, "If you have
judged me to be faithful to the Lord, come into
my house and stay." And she prevailed upon us.

ACTS 16:14–15 NASB

Lord, Lydia serves as an example for me. She was a wealthy woman, a dealer in purple cloth, and yet she was humble. She recognized her need for Jesus. She and her family were baptized, and then—immediately—she began a new life of service to You. She showed hospitality to servants of the Lord. I love the way the scripture says that Lydia's heart was opened. You opened her heart. You chose Lydia, Father, before the foundation of the world. And You chose me. Thank You for my salvation, and use me, as You used Lydia, to further Your kingdom, I pray. Amen.

God Sees the Heart

*But the LORD said to Samuel, "Do not look at
his appearance or at the height of his stature,
because I have rejected him; for God sees not
as man sees, for man looks at the outward
appearance, but the LORD looks at the heart."*

1 SAMUEL 16:7 NASB

———◆———

Heavenly Father, You see my heart. The way
You view people is so different from how others
view us or even how we see ourselves. Samuel
took one look at the oldest son of Jesse and as-
sumed he was the chosen one to be the up-and-
coming king. But You stopped him in that very
moment and corrected him. You don't judge
a person by his or her outward appearance or
stature, but by the heart. God, tonight I ask You
to purify my heart. See if there is any wicked
way in me. Root out bitterness and malice if
it lives within the recesses of my heart. I want
to be pleasing to You in every way. I love You,
Lord. Amen.

God Thinks of Me

How precious also are Your thoughts to me,
O God! How vast is the sum of them! If I
should count them, they would outnumber
the sand. When I awake, I am still with You.
PSALM 139:17–18 NASB

———◆———

Lord, You are always thinking of me. What a
sweet realization. When I am facing a trial, I am
not alone. When I am afraid or feel anxious, Your
thoughts are with me. The image in these verses
makes me think of an old, old woman who has
collected greeting cards her children have sent
her over the years. There are stacks and stacks of
them in boxes too numerous to even count. Her
whole entire home is full of them. They spread
out onto the rooftop and porches. Of course, this
is a silly exaggeration. But the number of greeting
cards in this little image does not begin to compare with the vast sum of Your thoughts about
me. You are always thinking of me. When I go
to sleep, You have me on Your mind. And when
I wake again, You are still thinking of me. I love
You, Lord. Thank You for thinking of me. Amen.

The Lord Knows Me Well

O LORD, You have searched me and known me.
You know when I sit down and when I rise
up; You understand my thought from afar. You
scrutinize my path and my lying down, and are
intimately acquainted with all my ways.

PSALM 139:1–3 NASB

Lord, private investigators have nothing on You.
You search and know and study me. You study
my paths. You watch over me as I lie down. You
are intimately acquainted with all my ways!
You are my Creator, and You know me better
than anyone does. You knit me together in my
mother's womb, and You have had Your eyes
on me ever since. Thank You for knowing me
so well. You never lose track of me. This brings
me comfort tonight. I love You, Lord. In Jesus'
name, amen.

The Promise of Eternal Life

And this is what he
promised us—eternal life.

1 JOHN 2:25 NIV

Heavenly Father, tonight I come praising Your name. I praise You for who You are. You are Alpha and Omega, beginning and end. You are the everlasting Lord, the King of kings, the Redeemer, my Savior, and friend. You have filled Your Word with promises I can count on. I stand firm in my faith, and Your promises fill me with hope. You have promised me an abundant life, and I know that for the Christian there is no real death. I will live eternally with You in heaven. I find contentment in that tonight, Lord. Although this world is a fallen one, there is hope of heaven. I will always have hurts, longings, and disappointment here on this earth. This world is imperfect. But You travel along with me, day by day, and my life is filled with victories and joys in spite of the struggles. One day there will be no more pain, only worship. There will be a new heaven and a new earth. I thank You tonight for the promise of eternal life. Amen.

The Promise of Heaven

"My Father's house has many rooms; if that were not so, would I have told you that I am going there to prepare a place for you? And if I go and prepare a place for you, I will come back and take you to be with me that you also may be where I am."

JOHN 14:2–3 NIV

———•———

Jesus, this passage reminds me of cause and effect. We learned it in school. "If-then statements," the teachers called them. You tell me that Your Father's house has many rooms. You say that *if* this weren't so, *then* You would not have said You were going there to prepare a place for me. And then You use another if-then. *If* You go to prepare a place for me, *then* You will come back for me. I cannot imagine heaven, and there are many mysteries about it. But what I do know is that there are many mansions there. It is a real place where people live—the people of God. And I know that one day I am going there. You are busy preparing a place for me there even now. As I go to sleep, I smile, imagining forever in paradise. Thank You for giving me this glimpse at the future. I love You, Jesus. Amen.

The Sheep Know Their Shepherd's Voice

*"My sheep listen to my voice; I know them,
and they follow me. I give them eternal life,
and they shall never perish; no one will
snatch them out of my hand."*

JOHN 10:27–28 NIV

Good Shepherd, I hear Your voice. I know You, and You know me. I follow after You and seek to stay on Your path. I am sometimes tempted to go astray. It is then that You come after me. You know no limits when it comes to Your little sheep. You call to me with Your loving voice. You protect me with Your staff and Your rod. You watch over me as I lie down to sleep. You are here on guard all night long. I do not have to fear the darkness because my Good Shepherd never sleeps or slumbers. Thank You for this type of protection, Father, that only You can offer me. No one is able to snatch me out of Your hand. You promise me that. May I always be able to discern my Shepherd's voice from the other voices that call to me in this world. I want to always follow You. I love You, Lord. Amen.

Faith

Now faith is confidence in what we hope
for and assurance about what we do not see.
This is what the ancients were commended for.

HEBREWS 11:1–2 NIV

———————•———————

Lord, it is easy to hope for what I see right before me. There is no mystery there. There is no faith required. It is simple to be assured of the concrete and visible. I don't have to trust You for these things. But You call me to faith. You call me to believe that You died on a cross even though I did not touch the scars in Your hands like Thomas. You ask me to believe that You died for me and that three days later, You rose again. I was not there to see the stone rolled away. You tell me You are coming again and that Christians will live forever in heaven with You. These are things I must believe without seeing—yet. Grow my faith, I pray. I am so thankful for Your promises. Amen.

My Plans and God's Plans

In their hearts humans plan their course,
but the LORD establishes their steps.

PROVERBS 16:9 NIV

———◆———

God, often I make plans for myself. We all do it to some degree. We map out our steps. We plan our lives like we plan a vacation—right down to the detail. Young girls plot out the age at which they will marry and when they will have each of their children. Some go so far as to name the children and write their names in journals or diaries! Years later, it is funny to look back at how we planned our lives. They usually turn out rather differently. You know the ways You have for us. You know the plans, and they are always plans for our good. Thank You, Lord, that although I am good at making plans, Your course for me always trumps the one I come up with! Your ways are perfect. May I trust in them as I go to sleep tonight. Amen.

He Gives Peace

*Now may the Lord of peace himself give
you peace at all times and in every way.
The Lord be with all of you.*

2 Thessalonians 3:16 niv

Lord of peace, You are the only one who is able to give peace. I love this passage that promises You give peace at all times and in every way to Your children. Like an all-you-can-eat dinner at a restaurant, there is an unlimited supply! When I am facing a deep sorrow or grief, You provide peace that sustains me. When I am weary, there is peace available to me. When I reach a dead end in life and cannot imagine how I will go on, You provide peace. You never run out, and You provide just the right version of peace that I need in each situation. I love You, Father, and I thank You for giving me peace. I ask that You wrap me up in Your peace tonight and sing over me as I drift off to sleep, secure in Your care. Amen.

The Great Physician

He heals the brokenhearted and
bandages their wounds.
PSALM 147:3 NLT

———◆———

Great Physician, You heal the brokenhearted.
Your Word says You bandage their wounds.
Find me here tonight. There are broken parts of
me. Some are newly inflicted wounds. Others I
have carried for a lifetime. On the surface, they
have scarred over and are hardly noticeable to
others. But the wounds are there. They run deep.
I have not forgotten because they stay with me.
Father, heal me. Just as the surgeon removes the
cancer. Just as the doctor puts a cast on the broken
bone to make it right again. You are the God who
sees. Just as You saw Hagar in the wilderness,
find me here, and bind up my wounds that I
might be healed completely and forever. In Jesus'
name I ask, amen.

A New Creation in Christ

This means that anyone who belongs
to Christ has become a new person.
The old life is gone; a new life has begun!
2 CORINTHIANS 5:17 NLT

Lord, You tell me I am a new creation in Christ. Like the caterpillar becomes a butterfly or the tadpole transforms into a frog, I have left behind my old self. I am new. Thank You for a new start. Thank You for giving me the Holy Spirit to guide me as I seek to walk in Your ways. I want to be pleasing to You in my actions and even in my thoughts. Remind me not to look back over my shoulder wishing I could change the past. Sometimes late at night my mind turns to the past, and I am filled with regret. Keep my eyes focused on the future. There is no strength or purpose in looking back. You will redeem the years eaten by locusts. You bring beauty from ashes. Thank You, Lord, for making me new. In Jesus' name, amen.

No Shame in Christ

*As Scripture says, "Anyone who believes
in him will never be put to shame."*

ROMANS 10:11 NIV

Lord, in You there is no shame. There are spots
in my life where I feel shame. I hang my head. I
want to hide. I feel embarrassed. I feel isolated
in my shame. But then You remind me that this
is not who I am. I am more than a conqueror
through Christ. I hold my head high. You are
the lifter of my head. My eyes are bright, and
I am filled with joy and newness of life. I come
out of my hiding place. My cheeks are not red.
My eyes meet those around me. I am a child of
the King. I am made righteous through Christ
Jesus. I live in community because I am a part
of the body of Christ. Nothing can separate me
from the love of God. Take the remaining bits
of shame from me tonight, Father. And, as I lay
my head down on my pillow tonight, whisper
to me that I am Your daughter, and though my
sins were as scarlet, You have made me white as
snow. Amen.

Christ Is the Cornerstone

God warned them of this in the Scriptures
when he said, "I am placing a stone in
Jerusalem that makes people stumble,
a rock that makes them fall. But anyone
who trusts in him will never be disgraced."

ROMANS 9:33 NLT

Jesus, You are the Cornerstone of the Church, causing some to stumble and others never to be disgraced. The religious leaders in Your day were so proud, but You clearly showed that there was no security to be found in self. I am thankful I know You as my Savior. I come to You tonight, great Cornerstone, and I need to sense You near. I need the security that You promise. I feel shaken, but I know that I need only look to You in order to gain my balance again. I stand strong and secure upon a firm foundation. I draw upon the strength You have given me in the past. I rest in Your righteousness. I curl up in Your arms like a child and lean against Your strength. In You I need never remain afraid. And when I am weak, it is then that You are strong. It is then that there is only "one set of footprints in the sand," because You carry me. Amen.

Looking Up!

I lift up my eyes to the mountains—where does my help come from? My help comes from the LORD, the Maker of heaven and earth.

PSALM 121:1–2 NIV

Lord, help me to remember to look up. My help comes from the Lord! Like a child's face turns up toward a parent, may I always remember that You are there to help me. May I turn my face toward You. May I look up. Father, so many times throughout my days and even as I go to sleep at night, I need Your help. I need Your help in decision-making and in keeping my calm. I need Your help as I navigate relationships and responsibilities. I need Your guidance. Father, thank You that I know where my help comes from. Remind me not to waste time posting my issues and problems on social media or texting every friend and family member about them. May I truly remember to come to You first with my needs. Thank You, Father, that I need only look up! Give me rest now, I ask. Amen.

Fix My Gaze upon God

I lift up my eyes to you, to you who sit enthroned
in heaven. As the eyes of slaves look to the hand
of their master, as the eyes of a female slave look
to the hand of her mistress, so our eyes look to the
LORD our God, till he shows us his mercy.

PSALM 123:1–2 NIV

———————•———————

God, I lift up my eyes to You. I keep my gaze
fixed upon You. Students must keep their focus
on the teacher. Servants must watch their master.
Children keep their gaze fixed upon their parents.
Even animals follow the lead of their owners.
Father, may my gaze be always fixed upon You.
It is when I am fully in sync with You that the
cares of this world fade away. My struggles seem
so small and my trials so trivial when I bask in
Your Word and in prayer. My time with You
cannot be pushed to last place each day. Help
me tonight to consider ways that I can save time
tomorrow, ways that I can make more time to
spend with my God. I love You, Lord. Your mercies are new every morning. Amen.

The Lord Is My Rescuer

*Praise be to the LORD, who has not let us be torn
by their teeth. We have escaped like a bird from
the fowler's snare; the snare has been broken, and
we have escaped. Our help is in the name of the
LORD, the Maker of heaven and earth.*

PSALM 124:6–8 NIV

Lord, You are my Rescuer. Point me back to that
truth tonight as I spend these quiet moments
with You. I look back over my life and see all
the times You showed Yourself faithful. You have
reached down and snatched me out of bad situa-
tions. You have allowed unhealthy relationships
to dissolve. You have given me strength when I
am weak, hope when I am depressed, and joy in
the midst of sorrow. Father, I am reminded of
the Israelites who passed through the Red Sea.
I think of the spies who were hidden by Your
servant, Rahab. Time after time, You have saved
the day for Your children. I praise You for Your
faithfulness. I recognize You as my great Helper.
What a blessing that the Creator of the universe
is also my Rescuer, my constant Protector. In
Jesus' name I pray, amen.

Solid Rock

Those who trust in the LORD are like Mount Zion,
which cannot be shaken but endures forever. As
the mountains surround Jerusalem, so the LORD
surrounds his people both now and forevermore.

PSALM 125:1–2 NIV

Heavenly Father, in this era when everything changes quickly, You are solid and secure. Through the ages, You have stood, like a mountain that cannot be shaken. Tonight I am exhausted from the busy pace of life in this world. There are so many demands on me as a woman. I rush through my days, and when I come home and find some rest and some quiet moments with You, I am reminded of Your sovereignty. Help me, Father, to seek You all throughout my day instead of just at its close. What strength You provide for me. You are my Rock. As I go to sleep tonight, bring to mind all the times You have been faithful in the past and bring over me a calm assurance that You are not going anywhere. You are in this for the long haul with me. You are never changing. You are never leaving. You are never giving up on me. What a comfort to know that my Rock is solid and sure. In Jesus' name I pray, amen.

Forgiving God

Out of the depths I cry to you, LORD; Lord, hear my voice. Let your ears be attentive to my cry for mercy. If you, LORD, kept a record of sins, Lord, who could stand? But with you there is forgiveness, so that we can, with reverence, serve you.

PSALM 130:1–4 NIV

Lord, You hear me. You come to me. You are never far away. Like the mother who shows up at a child's bedside when she hears his call, You show up. You care. You listen to me. You touch my weary brow and reach out and wipe the tears from my cheeks. You are gentle and loving. You forgive. If You did not forgive, just as the psalm says, who could stand? Certainly not I! What peace I find tonight even as my soul is weary. What peace is grasped when a believer recognizes that with You, Abba Father, there is forgiveness. There are do-overs. There are second chances. There is a chance to change and do better tomorrow. You are my God, my Redeemer, my friend, and I will praise You all of my days. Thank You for keeping no record of wrongs. Thank You for Jesus, who takes away my sin. In His powerful name I pray, amen.

Waiting for the Lord

I wait for the LORD, my whole being waits,
and in his word I put my hope. I wait for the
Lord more than watchmen wait for the morning,
more than watchmen wait for the morning.

PSALM 130:5–6 NIV

Lord, waiting has never been my forte. I am required to wait multiple times per day. I wait at intersections for the green light. I wait in the drive-through line for my fast food. I wait on others. I wait for answers. I wait. Sometimes I do it more successfully than others. Some days I can muster up a bit more patience. Other times, the waiting stretches me too far and I lose my cool! Father, help me now in the quiet of these moments spent with You before bed. Help me to learn to wait on You. Remind me that when You ask me to wait, it is always for my good. You may not be saying no. You may simply be saying, *"Wait."* You may simply be asking me to trust in Your timing and in Your perfect will. Give me the patience I so need in order to wait on Your best. In Jesus' name I pray, amen.

Contentment in the Lord

My heart is not proud, LORD, my eyes are not
haughty; I do not concern myself with great matters
or things too wonderful for me. But I have calmed
and quieted myself, I am like a weaned child with
its mother; like a weaned child I am content.

PSALM 131:1–2 NIV

———————

Lord, I confess that I fall short in the contentment
department! I ask You to fill me with a new level
of contentment. There will always be longing in
my life. I live in a fallen world. Things are not
perfect. I will always be able to look around and
find someone who appears to have it easier or
better than I do. Instill in me, I pray, a deep joy.
One that does not envy others or shift with circumstances but is solid and sure. Remind me that
true happiness does not come from this world. It
is only found in You. Help me to clear my mind
now in these final moments of the day. I love
You, Lord, and I want to be ever so content just
to live and breathe and make my being, just to
walk humbly with my God. In Jesus' name, amen.

Getting Along with Others

*How wonderful, how beautiful, when brothers
and sisters get along! It's like costly anointing oil
flowing down head and beard, flowing down
Aaron's beard, flowing down the collar of his
priestly robes. It's like the dew on Mount Hermon
flowing down the slopes of Zion. Yes, that's where
GOD commands the blessing, ordains eternal life.*

PSALM 133:1–3 MSG

Lord, the end of another day is upon me. Thank
You for seeing me through the ups and downs this
day has held. I confess that there were moments
in my interactions today that were not pleasing
to You. Give me a new start tomorrow, Father,
and a fresh perspective. Remind me that you
have made each of us in Your image. Show me
the good in each person that I deal with throughout the day tomorrow. I know that it is so pleasing to You when we get along as brothers and
sisters. In Jesus' name, amen.

Praying at Nighttime

Everyone who serves the LORD, come and
offer praises. Everyone who has gathered in
his temple tonight, lift your hands in prayer
toward his holy place and praise the LORD.

PSALM 134:1–2 CEV

———————•———————

Lord, I often hear or read that a quiet time should
be in the morning. While I find great benefit
in meeting with You first thing each day, I also
see the value in some quiet moments at nighttime. May I be found singing Your praises in the
morning and in the evening. As the children's
song says: "Jesus in the morning, Jesus at the
noontime, Jesus when the sun goes down. . ."
May I put you first in my life and may I seek
You early in the morning. May I also close my
day with You, remembering to praise You as I go
to sleep and ask You to watch over and protect
me in the night. I love You, Lord. In Jesus' name
I pray, amen.

Idols

*Idols of silver and gold are made and worshiped
in other nations. They have a mouth and eyes,
but they can't speak or see. They are completely
deaf, and they can't breathe. Everyone who
makes idols and all who trust them will
end up as helpless as their idols.*

PSALM 135:15–18 CEV

Lord, You are a living Lord. You are not a lowercase *g* god fashioned with human hands. The Bible warns those who worship such gods. They will end up as helpless as their idols. Father, keep my heart pure and focused on You. Protect me, I ask, from the lure of idols. They take many shapes, and many are not as obvious as the golden calf. Idols come in the form of time stealers like social media and even relationships. I am tempted to give my best to others. I am tempted to spend more time on them than I do in Your holy Word. Father, I am so thankful to know the one true God. Please keep me close. As I go to sleep, impress upon my heart the importance of putting You first. Amen.

Famous and Enduring Lord

Your name, O LORD, endures forever,
Your fame, O LORD, throughout all generations.
For the LORD will judge His people, and He
will have compassion on His servants.

PSALM 135:13–14 NKJV

———————

Lord, Your holy name will last forever. When there is a new heaven and a new earth, You will remain. When a million more suns have risen and set, You will remain. We will all give an account and stand before You. How thankful I am that when that day comes and I must stand before You, Holy God, I can claim the name of Jesus. He is my righteousness. Cause me to live in such a way as to bring more and more fame to Your glorious name. Father, make Yourself famous through my life. May I be known as one who stands on Your statutes and shares Your good news freely. As I drift off to sleep tonight, I am comforted that I serve a famous and forever God. Amen.

Mercies Unending

Oh, give thanks to the LORD, for He is good!
For His mercy endures forever. Oh, give thanks
to the God of gods! For His mercy endures
forever. Oh, give thanks to the Lord of lords!
For His mercy endures forever.

PSALM 136:1–3 NKJV

———◆———

Lord, You are so good. You are a good, good
Father. Your mercies endure forever. They never
run out, run dry, or run short. Your mercies are
unending. Each new morning I find out a little
more about You. You meet me in a new way.
You reveal Yourself in a sunrise or through an
encouraging word spoken by a friend. I find myself freed from an entangling sin. I look up and
find You have taken hold of a situation too big
for me. You have fought another of my giants. I
notice a child's innocence, a puppy's playfulness,
a flower's beauty. You are all around me. You are
in everything. I thank You, God. I praise You
for being who You are—faithful, faithful Father.
I thank You for the blessings You bestow upon
me. You shower me with them, merciful God. I
praise You. I thank you. I rest in You tonight and
in Your mercies that endure for all time. Amen.

Strong God

*To Him who struck Egypt in their firstborn, for
His mercy endures forever; and brought out Israel
from among them, for His mercy endures forever;
with a strong hand, and with an outstretched arm,
for His mercy endures forever; to Him who divided
the Red Sea in two, for His mercy endures forever;
and made Israel pass through the midst of it, for
His mercy endures forever; but overthrew Pharaoh
and his army in the Red Sea, for His mercy endures
forever; to Him who led His people through the
wilderness, for His mercy endures forever.*

PSALM 136:10–16 NKJV

God, the verbs of the Bible are strong. Some are
positive and others harsh. You see Your people
through impossible circumstances. You hide them
away inside a giant ark filled with animals while
the evil perish in a flood. You draw them out of
the belly of a great fish. You part waters of a sea
and lead them through on dry land. You take out
Your enemies. You turn them to pillars of salt. You
allow firstborns to die. You hit them between the
eyes with the stone of a young boy's slingshot. I
praise You for Your mercies and for being a strong
God, a God who takes care of business. Amen.

God Covers My Head in Battle

O God the LORD, the strength of my salvation,
You have covered my head in the day of battle. Do
not grant, O Lord, the desires of the wicked; do not
further his wicked scheme, lest they be exalted.

PSALM 140:7–8 NKJV

Lord, You cover my head as I go into battle daily.
You are better than any brass helmet! You watch
over me. You protect me from those who may
wish to harm me. Just as David sang praise to
You for shielding him from Goliath and Saul,
I give You praise for all the times in my life
You have protected me. I also imagine all the
times when I had no idea You were keeping me
from harm. You surround me with Your angels,
I know. God, David's enemies had armor bearers.
David had none. And yet he won the battles.
You were the difference maker. You were given
the glory. May You be given the glory in the
battles You win for me as well. All the days of
my life. And may I wake up tomorrow prepared
to fight the good fight with no fear because You
are covering my head. Amen.

Nighttime Prayer

LORD, I cry out to You; make haste to me! Give ear to my voice when I cry out to You. Let my prayer be set before You as incense, the lifting up of my hands as the evening sacrifice.

PSALM 141:1–2 NKJV

Father, hear my prayer. It is an evening sacrifice of sorts. I come to You. I cry out. I ask that You will meet me here. I can only approach You through Jesus. He is my mediator, my bridge, my access giver. I am privileged to call on You in prayer. Protect me through this night, I ask. Give me the grace it takes to live as a Christ follower in this world tomorrow. Protect me from evil, and lead me on paths far from temptations that would love to drag me down. Thank You for hearing my requests. May my prayers be pleasing to You. In Jesus' name I pray, amen.

Hidden Treasure

And if you look for it as for silver and search for it
as for hidden treasure, then you will understand
the fear of the LORD and find the knowledge of
God. For the LORD gives wisdom; from his mouth
come knowledge and understanding.

PROVERBS 2:4–6 NIV

———————

Heavenly Father, may I seek wisdom as if I am on a treasure hunt! May I search for it as I would hidden jewels or millions of dollars, for it is worth more than any amount of money. Father, wisdom is only found in You. May I seek it all of my days. You tell me in Your Word that if I seek for it diligently, You will give it to me. It is found in Your Word. I can possess great understanding and knowledge. You don't want to keep wisdom a secret. You long to pour it out upon your children, if we only slow down long enough to ask. Help me, as I read in Proverbs, to accept Your words and follow Your commands. Show me how to listen not just with my ears but with my heart. I love You, Father, and I long to possess the wisdom needed for each day. In Jesus' name I ask, amen.

Prayer for Rest and for the New Day

Let the morning bring me word of your unfailing love, for I have put my trust in you. Show me the way I should go, for to you I entrust my life. Rescue me from my enemies, LORD, for I hide myself in you. Teach me to do your will, for you are my God; may your good Spirit lead me on level ground.

PSALM 143:8–10 NIV

Lord, give me rest tonight, I pray. Help me to lay aside the day and all its worries. There are problems left unsolved. There are solutions not yet solidified. There are unanswered questions. But I choose rest. I choose trust. I choose to unplug and rest in You. Father, as I go into a new day, I ask that the morning will bring reminders that I am deeply and unconditionally loved by You. Direct my paths, Father, and protect me from snares I cannot see. Show me Your perfect will that I might walk in it. Keep my feet stable and secure. Lead me on solid ground. In Jesus' name I pray, amen.

Never Withhold Good

Do not withhold good from those to whom it is due, when it is in your power to act. Do not say to your neighbor, "Come back tomorrow and I'll give it to you"—when you already have it with you.

PROVERBS 3:27–28 NIV

———◆———

Lord, thank You for another day of life. Thank You for all the blessings You have bestowed upon me. I have everything I need and much of what I want. You give me good gifts. You entrust me with much, and I know that much is expected of me. Make me a humble steward who makes wise choices with all of my resources. Help me to always see my belongings and money as Yours. Help me to make decisions based on Your perspective, not a worldly one. The world may tell me that You help those who help themselves, but I know this is not found in scripture! You tell me to give when it is within my power. Help me to give of my time, talents, and resources. I know full well that you will replenish them all to beyond overflowing. Give me rest tonight, Father, and bring into my path tomorrow those who need my help. Amen.

God Weighs My Heart

A person may think their own ways are right,
but the LORD weighs the heart.

PROVERBS 21:2 NIV

———————•———————

Lord, You weigh the heart. You see beyond my good deeds to my motives. You are aware each time I act or speak for the applause of others rather than simply to bless them. You point out to me ways to walk humbly, ways to give and serve anonymously, behind the scenes. Cause me to be satisfied there and not eager to have my name in lights before the crowd. Father, make me one who is known for having been with Jesus. May my attitudes and my choices reflect my Savior's love and grace. When I am truly walking with You and when my heart is pleasing to You, I am so content. At the end of the day, I rest before You. It always feels so good when I can honestly say I did my best throughout the day. You see my heart. You weigh it. You will always find it imperfect. You are not looking for perfection, but for a heart turned toward the kingdom, a heart that honors You. Give me such a heart, I ask. Amen.

The Difference

Better to live on a corner of the roof than
share a house with a quarrelsome wife.

PROVERBS 21:9 NIV

———

Lord, I lay my head on my pillow tonight. I am tired. I am weary, and along with weariness is intermingled some degree of regret. There were times when I did not represent You well today. I reflect on those times. Did I need to make that comment? Could I have held my tongue? Why did I argue? Why did I push those buttons I knew would upset the person with whom I was conversing? I consider what will make the difference tomorrow. I know there is only one thing, and that is time spent with You. That is prayer. That is meditating on Your Word. That is asking You to walk with me ever so close all through the day. Meet me here in these moments before bedtime, Lord, and walk with me throughout the day tomorrow. Make the difference in my life. I want to be a woman who is more and more like Jesus each day. I love You, Lord. Amen.

God Is My Pleasure

Whoever loves pleasure will become poor; whoever loves wine and olive oil will never be rich.

PROVERBS 21:17 NIV

Father, be my great pleasure. May I find my joy and solace and contentment in You alone all the days of my life. May You satisfy every longing and fulfill every desire. Take away any taste for worldly pleasures that I may develop. I am faced daily with so many options, so many choices, so many temporal distractions. I long to please you, Lord. I do not want to waste one moment of one day on the things of this world. May I live in the world and walk and serve here, but not be found enamored by it. Wrap me up in Yourself. Cover me with Your wings. Shield me. Be all that I desire. I will walk with You all the days that You give to me. I will follow hard after You. You are a good, good Father. Your Word warns against the pleasures of the world. I know that true wealth and delight are found in You. I love You. Amen.

The Power of Words

Those who guard their mouths and their
tongues keep themselves from calamity.

PROVERBS 21:23 NIV

Heavenly Father, tonight I come before You aware of the power of my words. Please set a guard over my mouth, I ask. Help me as I go into tomorrow to be aware that my words can truly lift and heal, but they can also be destructive. I pray that even as I rest and reflect on my day, You will point out to me people in my life who could benefit from some words of encouragement. I want to be a vessel of Your love, Lord. I want my speech to help others and to build them up and never to tear them down. God, I know how much it means to me to be the recipient of kind words. May I be the giver of such admonitions as well. Help me to learn to filter my words through a God filter before they find their way out of my mouth. In Jesus' name I pray, amen.

A Woman of Prayer

When he came back, he again found them
sleeping, because their eyes were heavy.
MATTHEW 26:43 NIV

Jesus, Your disciples slept. How discouraging
it must have been to find them snoozing when
You were in such earnest prayer in the garden
that night. Again and again, they dozed off. You
really saw the weakness of humanity that night.
I would love to think that I would have been
different, that I would have been found alert and
in prayer. But I know myself all too well. I am
a sleeper too. My mind drifts when I pray. My
heart wanders. Lord, help me to make prayer a
great priority in my life. Help it to mean more
to me even than sleeping or eating. May I seek
You with my whole heart and at all times of the
day and night. May prayer become a priority.
May it be the entrée, not a side dish on the menu
of my day. I love You, Lord, and I want to be found
a woman of prayer, one whose life is characterized
by prayer. I want people to know that I have been
with Jesus. Amen.

Good Comes from Sleep

*So the LORD God caused the man to fall
into a deep sleep; and while he was
sleeping, he took one of the man's ribs
and then closed up the place with flesh.*

GENESIS 2:21 NIV

Lord, good things come from sleep sometimes. Certainly, I do not wish to be idle or lazy. But Father, I look at all the good that can come from sleep. While Adam slept, You brought about Eve. You took a rib from him and created his helpmate. In his struggle with You through the night, you gave Jacob a new name. You gave him a new heart. The Bible says you blessed him. I see that good can come from sleep. Give me refreshment, I pray, as I rest tonight. Visit me with wisdom and peace, I pray. May my sleep be beneficial in whatever ways You see fit. And when I wake, may I honor You better in the new day than I did in the previous one. In Jesus' name I pray, amen.

Listening to God

If anyone turns a deaf ear to my instruction,
even their prayers are detestable.

PROVERBS 28:9 NIV

———————•———————

Lord, tonight I come to you asking that you
fine-tune my ears to hear Your instruction. May
I not just hear but listen to Your words. May I
walk in Your truths. May I be led each day by You
and You alone. Father, just as a sheep knows its
shepherd's voice, I know my Lord's voice. May
I never forget it, and may my heart and mind be
so in sync with that voice that even when it is
still and small, I hear it loud and clear. Father,
hear my prayers. I pray that You will never find
my prayers detestable. I never want to be known
as one who turned a deaf ear to You. It is so easy
in this fallen world to begin to think more of
ourselves than we should. Humble me quickly,
Father, if I should attempt to take control. I want
You always at the wheel. I want You to steer
me in the direction I should go. May I always
listen to You and act accordingly. In Jesus' name
I humbly ask, amen.

Walking in Wisdom

Those who trust in themselves are fools,
but those who walk in wisdom are kept safe.

PROVERBS 28:26 NIV

———◆———

Lord, like a toddler seeking independence, I often insist on "doing it myself," don't I? And yet trusting in myself can get me into such trouble. Grant me wisdom, Lord. Show me how to walk in Your ways. Humble me, Father, that I might not think so much of myself but realize I am but flesh and bone. I am weak. In and of myself, I am nothing. Only through Christ within me is there any hope at all that I will make a right choice, select a right path, or live a right life. God, keep me safe on the paths of wisdom. If I start to trust in me, stop me in my tracks. Remind me that those who trust in You will mount up with wings as eagles. I love You, Lord, and I want nothing more than to walk in Your ways and be led by Your wise hand. In Jesus' name I pray, amen.

Content in Christ

*I am not saying this because I am
in need, for I have learned to be
content whatever the circumstances.*

PHILIPPIANS 4:11 NIV

Father, in this world that pushes me to do better,
work harder, succeed, climb the ladder, and outdo
my neighbor. . .it is hard to rest in what I have
and what I am. Show me that true contentment
is found in You. Impress upon my heart that my
identity is in Christ alone and not in my wealth
or status. If the job is boring, may I find contentment. If the road is rough, may I be content. If
the relationship ends, if the child turns his back,
if the friend fails me, may I still find joy in You.
You never change. You are the same yesterday,
today, and tomorrow. You are all I truly need.
May I go to sleep tonight a bit more content
than You found me. May I find the secret of
being happy regardless of situation, regardless
of circumstance. The secret is Christ, who gives
me strength. Amen.

Trust in the Lord

Young lions may go hungry or even starve,
but if you trust the LORD, you will
never miss out on anything good.

PSALM 34:10 CEV

Father, I trust in You. When the storm clouds come and overwhelm my soul, I look up. I look into Your eyes. I call on You. I rest in You. I have found You faithful in the storms before, and so, when the winds pick up, I lay down my work. I lay down my striving. I raise my arms. I ask You to carry me. You never say no. I lean in a little closer. I bury my face in Your chest. I hide my eyes and let You do the navigating. I cling to the One who can calm the storm, knowing that even if You don't, You will get me through it. I will never miss out on any good thing because I have learned to trust in You on good days and bad alike. You are my Rescuer, my hero, and my Abba Father. As I go to sleep tonight, increase my trust in You. Grow my faith, I pray. You are the Way, the Truth, and You are the life giver, Lord. Amen.

Desiring God over Wealth or Possessions

For the love of money is a root of all sorts of evil, and some by longing for it have wandered away from the faith and pierced themselves with many griefs.

1 TIMOTHY 6:10 NASB

———◆———

Father, I ask You tonight to renew my desire to spend time with You. Whether in the morning or evening or both, I benefit so much from quiet time in Your presence. Reading Your Word and meditating upon it fills me with hope, comfort, and inspiration to live a life that pleases You. I ask that you help me to remember that nothing in this world has that kind of value. Prayer is such a privilege! I am able to converse with the Creator of the universe in those moments. No amount of money and no possession could compare. Keep me from a love of money and things. Fill me up to the brim with a love for You and a desire to grow in my faith. In Jesus' name I pray, amen.

Inner Beauty

Your adornment must not be merely
external—braiding the hair, and wearing
gold jewelry, or putting on dresses; but let
it be the hidden person of the heart, with the
imperishable quality of a gentle and quiet
spirit, which is precious in the sight of God.

1 PETER 3:3–4 NASB

Lord, as I close this day with You, please remind me that my inner beauty is much more important than my outward appearance. You judge the heart. Father, I know that You created me. You knit me together in my mother's womb. You determined my hair color, skin tone, and even whether I have freckles or not! Help me to set a good example for younger women and girls as I speak about myself. If they always hear me complaining about aspects of my physical appearance, they will follow my lead and do the same. I don't want to pass along such a negative attitude. Help me to be thankful for the way I look because it was decided by my heavenly Father. Help me also to focus on developing a gentle, quiet spirit that pleases You far more than any outward adornment. Amen.

Good Works Prepared for Me

*For we are His workmanship, created in
Christ Jesus for good works, which God prepared
beforehand so that we would walk in them.*

EPHESIANS 2:10 NASB

Jesus, in You I was created for good works. These good works were prepared and determined by God before I was even born! That amazes me. I come before You tonight and ask that You will give me opportunities to fulfill my purposes on this earth. Help me to be quick to recognize and seize such opportunities. If I have my head down and my eyes on a cell phone or tablet all the time, I will miss the good works You have for me! Show me how to humbly serve people, following the example You set for me during Your ministry here on earth. I want to be more generous, more loving, and more others oriented than I have been in the past. With each passing day, I ask that You make me a bit more like You, my Savior. My good deeds are for Your glory. May my light shine before men that they might glorify my Father who is in heaven. Amen.

The Word of the Lord Stands Forever

The grass withers, the flower fades,
but the word of our God stands forever.

ISAIAH 40:8 NASB

———————•••———————

God, tonight I recognize that very little in this world is lasting. Grass withers. Flowers fade. But Your Word stands forever. It never changes. Its promises ring as true today as they did years ago. Its statutes stand strong and if followed, provide a firm foundation for life just as they always have. When my relationships shift or come to a screeching halt, I look to Your Word. It remains. When the job disappoints and the money runs out, Your Word is still there. Grow in me a deep desire to read and meditate upon the Bible. As I read the words of Your holy scriptures, they become part of me. I draw upon them throughout each day. When I am on the mountaintop, I remember to praise You because I am in the habit of meeting with You and dwelling upon Your word. When life takes me through a storm or plunges me into a valley, Your Word pulls me through, giving me the endurance I need to persevere. I love Your Word, Father, and I love You. Amen.

Spirit-Led Mind

So letting your sinful nature control your
mind leads to death. But letting the Spirit
control your mind leads to life and peace.
ROMANS 8:6 NLT

Holy Spirit, please control my mind. Meet me here tonight at the end of yet another day in this fallen world. Replace my worry with peace, my discouragement with hope, and my exhaustion with a renewed strength. I know the difference between life and death. I see it around me every single day. I see those who are lost, those who follow hard after Satan whether or not they know he leads them. I see those who seek their solace in the things of this earth and come up, again and again, empty handed. Fill me, instead, with the things of God. May my mind be controlled solely by You, dear Holy Spirit of the living. You will always lead me to life and to peace. It is in the name of Jesus I pray, amen.

Accessorizing with the Fruit of the Spirit

And I want women to be modest in their appearance. They should wear decent and appropriate clothing and not draw attention to themselves by the way they fix their hair or by wearing gold or pearls or expensive clothes. For women who claim to be devoted to God should make themselves attractive by the good things they do.

1 TIMOTHY 2:9–10 NLT

Dear God, my loving Father in heaven who is right here with me now, I love You. I love the way You love me. I am deeply loved and cherished exactly as I am. I need no special clothing or jewelry. My hairstyle matters not. You don't care where I buy my clothes. You want my devotion to You to be obvious through my actions, not my looks. Help me never to seek to draw attention to myself through the style of clothing or the type of accessories I choose. Father, instead may I seek to accessorize my life with kindness, patience, goodness, and peace. These are the traits that will draw others not to myself, but to my Father. My good, good Father who will satisfy their every desire and give to them abundant and eternal life. In Jesus' name I pray, amen.

Inside and Out

"Outwardly you look like righteous people,
but inwardly your hearts are filled
with hypocrisy and lawlessness."
MATTHEW 23:28 NLT

———————•———————

Lord, You were straightforward with the Pharisees. These men were supposed to be righteous, godly men. They were leaders and teachers of the law. And yet, they were hypocrites! Father, help me to be the same on the inside as I appear to be on the outside. May my life be characterized by kindness and love. I would never want to be known as one who wears Christian T-shirts and has an ichthys symbol on my car and yet cannot spare a dime for someone in need. May I shower others with grace and goodness the way you have done with me. May my actions represent You well. Keep me from hypocrisy. Keep me from lawlessness. May I be found the same on the inside as I am out the outside. May I reflect You in all that I do. I ask these things in the name of Jesus, amen.

Discretion and Understanding

Discretion will protect you,
and understanding will guard you.
PROVERBS 2:11 NIV

———————•—•———————

Heavenly Father, tonight I come to You in need of security. As a woman in this big world, sometimes I am afraid. I try to be aware of my surroundings when I go out alone at night. But there is always a hint of fear. Remind me that You are always watching over me. Just as You protect me physically, surrounding my home, car, and workplace with Your angels, I know You also protect and guard my heart. You tell me in Your Word that my heart is the wellspring of life. Help me to keep my heart safe from the world and its influences, secure in Jesus Christ. Give me discretion, Lord. Help me to easily determine that which I should let into my life and that which I should keep at a distance. Fill my mind with understanding and wisdom. Keep me secure beneath Your wing at all times, I ask in the name of Christ Jesus. Amen.

Never Forsake Wisdom

Do not forsake wisdom, and she will protect you;
love her, and she will watch over you.

PROVERBS 4:6 NIV

───────•───────

Heavenly Father, I could stand to forsake a lot
in this world. I could give up my indulgences
in food and movies. My life would probably
benefit from forsaking some of the time I waste
on social media or even reading too late into
the night. There is one thing I never want to
forsake, Lord—one thing that is a light unto my
path. That is wisdom. Wisdom comes to me only
from You. When I seek it, You are faithful to
provide it. When I pray earnestly to understand,
You guide me to knowledge far too vast for me
to have ever reached alone. May I be led by wisdom all of my days. I find protection as I hold
on to wisdom. I find security in it. Thank You for
that, Lord. Thank You for wisdom from heaven
that You generously gift me with when I seek it
with all of my heart. Amen.

Take Refuge in the Lord

But let all who take refuge in you be glad; let them ever sing for joy. Spread your protection over them, that those who love your name may rejoice in you.

PSALM 5:11 NIV

Lord, I find my refuge in You. You are a strong tower. You are my haven and my hiding place. I find great joy and security in You. I do not need to worry or fear because You are my God and You always take care of me. Tonight I ask that You spread your protection over me. Like a thick quilt in the coldest of temperatures, it warms me and keeps me from this frigid world and all of Satan's temptations. I love Your name, God. I rejoice in You regardless of my circumstances. On my best day, I will sing Your praise. And when I am experiencing trials and tribulations, I will yet praise You! As I go to sleep tonight, cover me in Your protection and remind me to always seek refuge in You alone. My hope is in You. In the name of Your precious Son, Jesus, I pray, amen.

Free in Christ

It is for freedom that Christ has set us free.
Stand firm, then, and do not let yourselves
be burdened again by a yoke of slavery.

GALATIANS 5:1 NIV

———•———

Christ Jesus, I am free. I thank You for setting me free. How silly it would be for me to turn back and take up a yoke of slavery again. What an unnecessary burden that would be! I am free—free to live. I am free to serve and give. I am free to worship in the way that You lead me. I am free from legalism. I am free from religion. Instead, I am blessed with relationship. I am free from the past. You call me a new creation! I am free to walk humbly with my neighbors and to live at peace to the best of my ability. I am free from worry and anxiety. I am free even from death, for there is no real death for the Christian. You have removed the sting of death for me. I will pass from this life to eternity with You. Thank You, Jesus, for purchasing my freedom from sin on the cross. I will be eternally thankful for his freedom known only through Your blood. Amen.

Walking in Step with the Spirit

Since we live by the Spirit,
let us keep in step with the Spirit.
GALATIANS 5:25 NIV

Holy Spirit, may I walk in step with You. Just as a little child places his feet on top of his daddy's and smiles as they walk along together, may I be in tune with where You lead me. May I never attempt to run ahead or in a different direction. May I seek You and follow You. In Your timing, You will show me the way. May I never lag behind or doubt Your ability to direct me on the correct paths. I know that You only have my best interest at heart. Help me to walk in step with You tomorrow and the next day and the day after that. As I journey through life, I will look to You for direction. You have shown me so many times in the past exactly what route to take. I will trust that You will show up again and again as my compass and my map. Spirit, lead me to deeper waters that I may trust in You even more. Amen.

Kindhearted Woman

A kindhearted woman gains honor,
but ruthless men gain only wealth.
PROVERBS 11:16 NIV

Lord, there are many adjectives that might describe a woman. There are *ruthless* women who make great business deals and gain wealth but make no friends along the way. They leave a path of destruction. Their word means nothing. They don't know You. There are *weak* women. These women hide in the shadows. They don't live life. They are afraid to live for You. They know You, but they keep You to themselves. They are too shy to share. There are *busy* women, Father. This is a common word today. Busy. So many women are busy! They are so busy that they miss a lot. They look up and their children are grown, their hair is gray, their lives have passed, and they have nothing to show for it all. Father, there is an adjective for women in Proverbs 11:16. I would love to be known as a *kindhearted* woman. Show me opportunities to be kind. As I go to sleep tonight, remind me of Your kindness to me. You pour it out day and night. You love me, and You are so very kind. Make me a *kindhearted* woman, I pray. Amen.

Protect Me from the Temptation to Gossip

Women must also be serious. They must not gossip or be heavy drinkers, and they must be faithful in everything they do.

1 TIMOTHY 3:11 CEV

———

God, keep me from gossip, I pray. It is a constant trap, seeking to lure me in with a juicy tidbit. It has the ability to make me feel better about myself as I assist in putting down another woman. It attracts me with its half-truths. Gossip is so appealing. I cannot determine why. I think it goes back to the garden. I imagine Eve lusting after that fruit. She longed for the forbidden. Like the crunch of that Eden apple, gossip echoes through my texts and phone calls. It is information I am not to know, and yet I do. It is told to me in secret. It is whispered just as the serpent seduced Eve, with phrases like "I am telling you out of concern. . . ." Gossip masquerades behind counterfeit sympathies such as "Bless her heart." It spreads like a virus. It infects everyone in its path. Be my inoculation. Immunize me from the poison of gossip, I ask in the powerful name of Jesus. Amen.

God Reaches Down

He reached down from on high and took
hold of me; he drew me out of deep waters.
PSALM 18:16 NIV

———

Lord, You are holy. You are God on high, and yet
You choose to reach down. You reached down and
became a servant Savior, born in a stable, laid in
a manger for Your bed. You could have come as
a royal king adorned with jewels and riding in a
grand chariot. And yet You chose to reach down
and become one of us. You reached down and
saved me from sin. You hung upon a cross and
died the death of a criminal that I might receive
life abundant and eternal. Tonight I come before
You asking You to reach down yet again. Reach
down and save me from deep waters that threaten
to drown me. At times they are the deep waters of
depression. At times they are deep waters I have
gotten myself into by dismissing Your warnings
and diving in anyway. I ask You to look past my
failure and reach down. Save me, Lord, once
again. Amen.

Peace Is Found in the Lord

"The LORD bless you and keep you; the LORD make his face shine on you and be gracious to you; the LORD turn his face toward you and give you peace."

NUMBERS 6:24–26 NIV

———— ◆ ————

Lord, I come to You tonight asking for Your blessing. Make Your face shine upon me. Be gracious to me yet again, I ask. Turn Your face toward me, and give me peace tonight. I am so in need of Your peace. You know the worry within me that I struggle so deeply to relinquish to You. Tonight it keeps me awake again, tossing and turning. Take it from me, I pray. Cause me to loosen my grip on it. Remind me that You are big enough, strong enough, and steady enough to handle any problem. I rest easy tonight. I breathe a sigh of relief. I let go. Again. And I find peace that passes all understanding. Amen.

Burden Bearer

Give your burdens to the LORD, and he
will take care of you. He will not
permit the godly to slip and fall.
PSALM 55:22 NLT

I am not meant to bear my own burdens, Father. I know that is a lie the prince of darkness tries to sell me. I will reject it. Hear my cries tonight. See the worry that consumes me. Help me to cast my cares upon You and not scurry to pick them up and carry them myself again. You are stronger than I am, and my burdens are not overwhelming to You as they are to me. Carry them for me. Help me to stand up straight again, unencumbered by this giant load. Free me of these cares that cloud my vision for the future. Make my steps light and my eyes bright and carefree again. Sort out my troubles for me. I know You love me and You want to be my burden bearer tonight and tomorrow and all of the days of my life. Give me the courage that it takes to trust You. Give me the strength to lay my worries down. In Jesus' name I ask, amen.

Assurance and Peace

"Don't let your hearts be troubled.
Trust in God, and trust also in me."

JOHN 14:1 NLT

———◆———

Lord, You know I am afraid tonight. I cannot hide my fear from You. You know me through and through, for You knit me together in my mother's womb. You knew me before I knew You. You have called me Your own, and that will never change. Nothing is able to snatch me from Your hand. You long for me to bring every worrisome thought captive before You. Teach me to allow You, Father, to replace fear with assurance and anxiety with peace. I know that I must make the choice to step toward you. I must choose to truly cast my cares upon You. Like the disciples during a raging storm on the boat, I admit to You that my faith wavers. It is sure one moment but lacking the next. Lord, increase my faith. You stand ready to help, ready to rescue, and ready to comfort. May I once and for all release all my troubles to You. Teach me to trust You, for I know that You will never let me down. Amen.

Run to the Lord

"He will wipe every tear from their eyes. There will be no more death or mourning or crying or pain, for the old order of things has passed away."

REVELATION 21:4 NIV

———●———

Lord, one day grief will be a thing of the past. I will hardly remember it, and I will never again experience its weight. In heaven, death and pain will cease to exist. There will be no more tears. But that is in the future when I am with You in glory. This is not my human experience. My losses are no small matter. They have cut me to my core and left me questioning Your love for me. Help me to sense and know and trust that You have not removed Your hand from my life. I know that You love me and that You always will. Tonight, I choose to run toward You in my grief—not away from You, Lord. In my mourning, I am weak, but You are strong. I will lean on You as my Comfort and my Strength tonight and in the days to come. In Jesus' name I pray, amen.

Comforting Others as I Have Been Comforted

Who comforts us in all our troubles, so that we can comfort those in any trouble with the comfort we ourselves receive from God.

2 CORINTHIANS 1:4 NIV

———◆———

Lord, help me to forgive and love as I have been forgiven and loved. Help me to comfort others as I have received comfort from Your hand. When I see another weary soul, bring to mind how it felt to feel Your hand of comfort upon my brow. You showed up for me. Help me to show up for them. Give me just the right words to help them, and at times let there be no words at all. Sometimes just showing up and standing beside someone is enough. You have brought me so much comfort in my times of need. You have turned sorrow into joy again. Help me to look to my left and right and see weary souls. Help me to be there for them, Father, as You are there for me. As I sit before You quietly tonight, bring to mind those in my circles who need to find comfort. Help me to comfort them and point them to You, the Great Comforter. Amen.

The Lord Is My Healer

When she heard about Jesus, she came up behind him in the crowd and touched his cloak, because she thought, "If I just touch his clothes, I will be healed." Immediately her bleeding stopped and she felt in her body that she was freed from her suffering.

MARK 5:27–29 NIV

Lord, the woman reached out to touch the hem of Your robe. What faith she had! She had suffered a bleeding disease for twelve long years. She came to You in desperation. She had heard of You. She had heard You were the Son of God and that You could heal her. And she trusted that. She trusted it enough to risk being noticed. She trusted it enough to reach out for help. I bear burdens tonight. I carry them even though they are heavy. I have experienced great loss. I carry anger and bitterness, and sometimes it overtakes me. Do I believe as the woman did? Do I believe that You can heal me, that You can lift the burden, that You can make me whole again? Draw me close, Lord. Give me courage to reach out and touch You. Be my Healer, I ask tonight. Amen.

Temporary Trials

I consider that our present sufferings
are not worth comparing with the
glory that will be revealed in us.

ROMANS 8:18 NIV

———————

God, I know life on earth is temporary. When I pass through the veil to the other side, I will experience the glory of heaven. Then I will see fully what I can only understand in part right now. In the midst of my present trial, remind me that this pain is temporary, but my life is eternal. My suffering will seem like nothing once I enter the magnificent mansion in heaven that Jesus has gone to prepare for me. Impress upon me that this choice of the narrow path is worth it. In the blink of an eye one day glory will be revealed, and I will never look back to life on earth where things were imperfect and broken. When I am in paradise with You, all things will be right. For now, I will choose to trust in You and allow You to carry me through this trial. Give me the peace that I need tonight in order to rest easy even though I know the trial will still be here in the morning. Help me to face it with grace and endurance in Jesus' name. Amen.

Staying the Course

Work willingly at whatever you do, as though
you were working for the Lord rather than for
people. Remember that the Lord will give you
an inheritance as your reward, and that
the Master you are serving is Christ.

COLOSSIANS 3:23–24 NLT

Lord, sometimes my work can be discouraging. I feel as if I am stuck doing a meaningless task day in and day out. I try not to wonder why You are leaving me in this position. But I know I must remember that I am in this position for a reason and that I must do the work set before me, day by day. I will encounter people I can share the Gospel with, people who need encouragement, and those who need to sense Your love. I can love the people I work with and those who pass through my workplace in a unique manner, because of the gifts and abilities You have given me. As a Christian, I am not just working for an earthly supervisor—I am always working for You, Lord. Help me to do my best and to work as if I am working for You. I know there is great reward in staying the course with You. Amen.

Come Boldly before the Throne

*Let us then approach God's throne of grace with
confidence, so that we may receive mercy and
find grace to help us in our time of need.*

HEBREWS 4:16 NIV

Heavenly Father, what a blessing that as I come
to You for help, I may come boldly. I am Your
daughter, saved by grace, and You want nothing
more than to provide the mercy and strength I
need. Tonight I seek Your help. I need You. I don't
have to hang my head in shame. Jesus' blood at
Calvary covered that shame. You see me through
a Jesus lens. You don't see my imperfection, but
instead, His righteousness. Because of Jesus, "it
is finished"; because He died for my sins, I can
come before Your holy throne of grace with my
head held high. You wipe my tears dry. You give
me courage for another day. You help me even
through this night. I will linger here a few moments, Lord, in the stillness and silence. I will
linger in Your presence at the foot of Your throne
and rest my weary head upon Your lap. Thank
You for the assurance that You are my King and
that You are always at work in my life. Amen.

Cling to the Good

Love must be sincere.
Hate what is evil; cling to what is good.
ROMANS 12:9 NIV

Lord, as this day closes, I dwell upon the good and ask for Your help in laying aside that which was negative. Each day brings with it something that I can celebrate—even if it is a small victory. I woke up this morning. I was able to get out of bed. I heard birds chirping or saw flowers in bloom. Teach me to love with a sincere heart, I ask. I long for my mind to be transformed so that I might be more grateful. Make me aware of that which is good in my life and help me to cling to it. Evil weighs me down, but love and goodness lighten my load. Thank You, Father, for Your Word that inspires me to cling to the good. In Jesus' name I pray, amen.